Praise for *Live* and Mary Anne Radmacher

"Mary Anne Radmacher has written a book of beauty, creativity, wisdom, and great good will. Her chapter on forgiveness alone is worth the price of the book."

—Hugh Prather, author of *Morning Notes* and *The Little Book of Letting Go*

"Many years ago, I bought a framed poster of 'Live with Intention,' the inspiring phrase by Mary Anne Radmacher. It has hung on my wall ever since, in seven different houses. I have since bought and read every book she has written. Mary Anne's newest book is beautiful, artistic, inspiring, and written from her heart."

—Dr. Patrick Williams, master certified coach and coauthor of *Becoming a Professional Life Coach: Lessons from the Institute for Life Coach Training* and *Total Life Coaching: 50+ Life Lessons, Skills, and Techniques to Enhance Your Practice and Your Life*

"*Live with Intention* showed up at the perfect moment in my life, when I needed to be reminded to recommit to 'the promises I make to myself.' This book is filled with wisdom and can be read daily as a reminder that we create our lives each day, anew. Mary Anne graciously shares her philosophy and her life stories to show us the way to a life crafted by choices. This book is a treasure chest of ideas which will empower and enrich your future."

—Gail McMeekin, LICSW, author of *The 12 Secrets of Highly Creative Women* and *The Power of Positive Choices*

"Mary Anne Radmacher is the messenger of our hearts. And *Live with Intention* is the perfect message for this moment."

—Janet Conner, author of *Writing Down Your Soul: How to Activate and Listen to the Extraordinary Voice Within*

"Accessible, grounded, joyful, and wise, Mary Anne Radmacher's *Live with Intention* is a pure gift, especially if you're looking for a practical yet visionary map of contemporary life. Pick up this gem and bask in insight after insight, all of which are solidly based on the realities of twenty-first century life. And it always seems like you're simply chatting with your best friend. Great graphics, too."

—David Kundtz, author of *Awakened Mind: One-Minute Wake Up Calls*

"*Live with Intention* should be within easy reach of every person who has ever dared to dream. It gives us the tools to believe we can go after those dreams and actually capture them. It is a tool for living life to the fullest."

—Pat Ballard, author of *10 Steps to Loving Your Body (No Matter What Size You Are)*

"*Live with Intention* is a wonderful guide for anyone who wants to make every day count. Mary Anne takes the hand of readers and guides them on a fantastic journey to living a passionate life."

—Loren Slocum, author of *The Greatest Love* and *Life Tuneups*

"Mary Anne Radmacher offers so much concise and powerful inspiration in this book that I was torn between finishing it or running out the door to begin living more intentionally this very minute. Quotes from the author, as well as from wise ones of the past, interspersed with Radmacher's text leave the lucky reader holding a gem worthy of a permanent spot on the nightstand."

—Kathleen Everett, RN, BSN, author of *Heart Knocks*

"Mary Anne Radmacher has created yet another powerfully positive call to action. Inspiring and straightforward, practical and divine— *Live with Intention* is all of this and more. This is a book that is not only a pleasure to read for the first time, but one I look forward to rereading again and again."

—Christine Mason Miller, author of *Ordinary Sparkling Moments*

"Mary Anne's writing and, more importantly, her life embrace and exude and extol intention. We are now gifted with an exquisitely inspirational and utterly practical guide for doing the same in our own lives. *Live with Intention* is a breath of fresh, life-giving air; one that at times soothes and calms us and at times engages and energizes us to be fully present in this moment and to expect the very best from the precious next. What an extraordinary treasure of a book!"

—Deanna Davis, PhD, author of *Laugh, Cry, Eat Some Pie*

"A book of heaven for our small days."

—Ruth Forman, author of *Prayers Like Shoes*

"Anyone who has ever met Mary Anne Radmacher knows that there are countless things to love and admire about her. She's a beautiful human being who gives generously from her heart and who genuinely lives everything she teaches. She's also absolutely delightful, with a childlike wonder that is infectious. (Think polka dots!) But in this moment, what I want to appreciate most about Mary Anne is her self-proclaimed devotion to being a poet and aphorist. In *Live with Intention* Mary Anne has given us another big, juicy basket filled with delectable (and easily digestible) truth fruits. Open the book anywhere and you will be gifted with yummy wisdom from Mary Anne and friends. There's lot to enjoy right now—and plenty to put in your pockets when you're hungry for more later! Set an intention right now to live the joyful practices gifted to you in this book!"

—Sherry Richert Belul, author of *Say it Now: 33 Creative Ways to Say I Love You to the Most Important People in Your Life*

"Mary Anne's work saved my life in 2003. After the loss of my mother, I was spiraling down and had no focus and no sense of ME. I had no idea that on my mom's birthday, which was two months after her death, that I would receive my first sense of healing through Mary Anne's verse 'We Laugh to Survive.' My mom was speaking to me, Mary Anne was speaking to me, and after a two hour meltdown in her booth... I was speaking to my soul to recover. I have represented Mary Anne's work since that day at my business in Charleston, South Carolina, and that same event will happen at my booth on almost a daily basis. Her verses open those floodgates for grief, fear, and those challenges with friends, family, and work. This connection then transfers to me to hear their story and I then become a conduit to help them find inspiration for themselves or family or friends. It has been an honor to handle Mary Anne's work and help so many people find confidence, courage and a sense of purpose in their journey in life."

—Owners of JOYCE's CHOICES

Live with Intention

Live with Intention

Remember and Do What Matters

Mary Anne Radmacher

Conari
Press
Mango Publishing
CORAL GABLES

Published by Conari Press, an imprint of Mango Publishing Group, a division of Mango Media Inc.

Cover Design and Layout: Roberto Núñez

For permission requests, please contact the publisher at:
Mango Publishing Group
2850 S Douglas Road, 2nd Floor
Coral Gables, FL 33134 USA
info@mango.bz

For special orders, quantity sales, course adoptions and corporate sales, please email the publisher at sales@mango.bz. For trade and wholesale sales, please contact Ingram Publisher Services at customer.service@ingramcontent.com or +1.800.509.4887.

Live with Intention: Remember and Do What Matters

Library of Congress Cataloging-in-Publication number: 2020940931
ISBN: (print) 978-1-64250-296-1, (ebook) 978-1-64250-297-8
BISAC category code: SEL021000, SELF-HELP / Motivational & Inspirational

Printed in the United States of America

To Gillian and Matt,
the founders and innovators at Quotable Cards

Thank you for including my words in the work you do in the world. You took your love of words and invited mine into your company's collection with graphic beauty and immediacy. I am grateful to you for broadcasting my words around the world and letting them keep such luminous and inspiring company.

LIVE WITH INTENTION.
WALK TO THE EDGE.
LISTEN HARD.
PRACTICE WELLNESS.
PLAY WITH ABANDON.
LAUGH. CHOOSE WITH NO REGRET.
CONTINUE TO LEARN.
APPRECIATE YOUR FRIENDS.
DO WHAT YOU LOVE.
LIVE AS IF THIS IS ALL THERE IS.
-MARY ANNE RADMACHER-

DESIGN BY QUOTABLE CARDS, INC.
*Used with permission. Shown in black and white.

"Step well the path of remembering lit by
the stars you have placed, with intention,
in the canopy of your own night sky."

—Mary Anne Radmacher

"A goal is a thing you decide to do. It has a
measured result and an ending. An intention is an
established motivation that guides you to your goal.
It is boundless and only ends when you do."

—Mary Anne Radmacher

Table of Contents

Author Note

Thank you for holding this book in your hand, and putting it in front of your eyes.

Those who loved the first release of *Live with Intention: Rediscovering What We Deeply Know* will find that this is so more than a rerelease. A lot of my life has changed in the last decade, and so have the contents of this book, including the subtitle "Remember and Do What Matters" and the addition of a Part Two self-guided course.

I am grateful to Mango Publishing for providing the opportunity to enjoy another dance with this volume.

The Parts of This Book

This book was first written ten years ago. In this reimagined volume, I bring the lessons and experiences of the last ten years of my life to its pages. These years have added two lines to my original poem as it was first composed decades ago: fail with enthusiasm, and lead and follow a leader. Each chapter holds my reflections on the meaning of each line. While this book can certainly be read start to finish, it's more impactful taken in small sections or opened randomly. The contents do not reflect a chronological order but rather the organic manner in which insight and purpose rise up in seemingly ordinary moments. I write in metaphor, in prose, in poem, in story. I share the stories of friends and meaningful words from others who have influenced me. Each chapter, in Part One, opens with commentary from someone who has been influenced by the "Live with Intention" poem over the years. This book follows the time-honored practice of a commonplace book. It is a gathering and a distillation of some of the most meaningful lessons and tales of my life. It is intended to inspire and uplift.

***

I am primarily a poet and aphorist. I write most readily in an essay form. I hope that makes it possible for you to open this book anywhere and read for a brief period of time and have something that you can reflect on or consider. I hope you will treat the book as a reference, write in the margins, and utilize my writing as fodder for your own writing. Peppered throughout the chapters are metaphor, stories, and whimsical letters to engage your imagination and provide a deeper view into that particular phrase in my manifesto of intentional living.

***

In Part Two, you'll find the curriculum for a twenty-two-day, or if you prefer, twenty-two-step, guided process. Perhaps you have a friend with whom you would enjoy having conversations or following the "remember and do what matters" process together. That process, once completed, allows you to identify the things that you want to consistently do, the things that awaken your core commitments. Many people call these their "key result areas." I call them the things that matter. In a practical sense, *they are your intentions.*

***

This book in both of its iterations is the result of actively living out what I believe. I do not write speculatively. I write from my experience and share that as candidly and vulnerably as I am able. My life is not perfectly ordered, nor am I without challenges or difficulties. I actively commit to apply and assess these thirteen components in each of my days. Some days contain more of them than others. Balance and ease of cadence do not always come easily to me, and that is why I have created systems over the course of my life to help bring clarity and balance to my days. I use the systems that I teach because they help me make sense of my life; they elevate my mindfulness about what is truly important to me. Utilizing these identified intentions in my 1,440 daily minutes helps me finish my day with a sense of contentment and satisfaction. I learn to celebrate the ways in which I have been successful in those minutes and to forgive the deficits where I have fallen into forgetting. Every day, another beginning.

***

Please consider my words. Take what works for you and leave the rest. I hope these words accompany you on the journey to more readily live your intentions and to remember and do what matters. Perhaps, if I am blessed with the opportunity, I'll update this book in another ten years!

Part I

Live with Intention

Introduction

"If we do everything else but that one thing, we will be lost. And if we do nothing else but that one thing, we will have lived a glorious life."

—Rumi

live with intention.
walk to the edge.
listen hard.
practice wellness.
play with abandon.
fail with enthusiasm.
laugh.
choose with no regret.
continue to learn.
lead and follow a leader.
appreciate your friends.
do what you love.
live as if this is all there is.

This poem, all forty-six words of it, summarizes how I aspire to live my life. These thirteen directives enliven me, improve my mindset, and make my heart sing when I am applying them to my task list, my goals, my embrace of each day, and how I travel regardless of where I go. I take Rumi's reference "If we do nothing else but that one thing, we will have lived a glorious life" to encompass the whole of my intentions that make it possible for me to remember and do what matters.

Here you will find stories about my experiences and those of some of my friends. As each of these directives come into play with my days and my priorities, you will find a process that has guided countless folk to arrive at their own conceptual collection that makes up their "one thing"—the stars in their own night sky. You'll come to a set of prompts designed to support you as you articulate your intentions. Perhaps you will specify for the first time what your motivating intentions are! People around the world have adopted this poem as their own manifesto for living. You are welcome to that as well. Placing focus on any one of these elements, or alternatively defining your own, will enrich your experience with the 1,440 minutes that make up each of your days.

Remembering. Yes. It is easy to drift into forgetting: forgetting our personal priorities, the things that animate the hours of our days and deliver our fundamental joys. We roll into the habit of meeting the expectations of others, seeking approval by fitting in, and, in general, responding to a status quo that does not necessarily resonate with our own intentions and goals. How can we remember those things that have inadvertently either been set aside in favor of going with a majority, disregarded, or last on a list? Defining and remembering your own intentions allows you to more readily embrace the things that really matter to you. Knowing your own intentional elements allows you to offer an unfettered *yes* to opportunities and an unapologetic *no* to others.

Intention. Goal. What's the difference? A goal is a destination, a place toward which you move. An intention is how you walk to that place. Your intentions are the way you navigate your way to the shores of each goal. Neither an intention nor your collection of intentions are a plan. They are *how* you plan. They determine what you choose to plan for!

Rooted Deeply

The tree is an ideal iconic image for the partnership between intentions and goals. Goals often reference remembering and doing what matters. Your intentions are the root system. A root system remains unseen yet makes all that is visible possible. While the roots are most often hidden, they support everything that grows out of them. The tree trunk is representative of your process of remembering what matters, and the branches, fruit, and blossom are the doing. The manifestation of all of these begins by being deeply rooted in your intentions, not with an overlay of the expectations of others nor accidental adherence to cultural norms, but a complete alignment with your roots, your intentions, and with the choices and actions you take. Every. Single. Day.

***

Most trees root deeply. What we see is the trunk, the branches, the leaves. We see how they bend in the wind. Supporting all that is seen is what we cannot see—roots that deepen as the rings add to the stories that circle outward each year. We do not see the roots that deepen and make the strength of improbable bending possible. The anchor of year following year, story after story, enables the tree to stand up, rise ever up, and oxygenate the world. Trees, rooted deeply, get so little credit for the work they do in the world. Your intentions, which make so much possible, are also often overlooked.

***

Our intentions are like those roots: unseen, yet supporting all the growth, often in spite of poor soil. Rooting deeper making it possible for the trunk to expand and branches to yield whatever growth or fruit is in its makeup. Our intentions inform our remembering. They frame how we consider our past and allow it to shape us and, minute by minute, they form the choices that we will make.

***

I want to provoke and inspire you to rediscover—to remember—that which you know deeply within your soul. I want to support your journey as you remember what you have overlooked or forgotten. Whether you remember yourself back to your own deeply held intentions or if in the alternative you use the ones identified in this poem, utilizing them as you work your way through your days will restore, renew, and bring to the forefront a life that is rich in meaning and easy enthusiasm. If you are already living such a life, mindfully applying your intentions even more deeply will generate results that will delight you. You will further animate and invigorate your days by holding your intentions in an even higher regard.

***

Intentions for the day gather like theater goers in line eager for the best seats at opening night. Intentions! Get yourselves together! Every morning is an opening curtain. Every day is opening night. Every night is that last performance of its kind that you will ever know—never to be seen again in just that way. Every intention held truly in the heart is painted on the walls of your soul. It is present on every road, at each intersection, at the ready for the time to travel on with you and reward you with the grace of actions aligned with your intentions.

Be You, the More You, the Better

Please note I do not suggest that you need to recreate yourself or in some way seek to be other than who you are. Being clear on your intentions enables you to be more of who you already are. It doesn't require you to be different than yourself, it means that you are more yourself. I shared with my friend, artist and professor Pat Wiederspan Jones, that becoming some imagined ideal is so overrated. In fact, I think it can be harmful. Deepening your ways has measurable value as long as it is in partnership with contentment. From every phase of life, the betterment voices whisper in our ears. Compelled by their voracious hunger and the industry that hunger has generated, they hiss the words, "More," "Faster." "Better," or "New and Improved." On especially ravenous days those voices declare, "Not nearly enough.

Do it several more times and make sure the last one is perfect. We only deserve your 100 percent, your absolute best." Such demands as these are often met with uncomfortable compliance. In so many instances you believed you had delivered your best offer—only to be met with the insatiable command, "Do it again, and THIS time, do it right." Eventually it becomes an expectation that there is always a higher level of achievement, if only you can outperform yourself a bit more. It's a real celebration when you stop inviting those betterment voices to all of your parties. Once you understand where continual improvement is required and the place where "good enough" is indeed good enough, it becomes easier to not be compelled by those voices. Once those insidious whisperers anticipate you will say something like, "Stop whispering to me," they'll show up less often. Once contentment rises in you and you are clear on the intentions that are your true measure, there's less of a chance you'll be able to hear them even if they do try and show up. When you are at ease with the intentions that propel you in your life, you can experience the ease of contentment.

***

Contentment recognizes that the only control it exerts is over itself. Contentment accurately observes that it may compose an orchestration but how the individual parts are played is well beyond its control. So contentment sings a song of its own choosing and travels along, sometimes humming, toward a vision known only to itself. Contentment understands that ambition, vital effort toward specific desires, is an essential element to walking toward a certain goal. It understands Les Brown, Jr.'s aphorism differently than most. "Shoot for the moon. Even if you miss, you'll land among stars." This does not imply blind acceptance of some destiny. Contentment recognizes options to consider. Meeting the goal of shooting for the moon is a single objective. Making it to the stars just means that there's less distance to travel the next time contentment tries for the moon, if making it to the moon is still a goal. Contentment is able to evaluate the view from among the stars. And, while it was not the initial objective, contentment has the capacity to embrace being among the stars as an even better outcome than what was initially planned.

***

My friend, Caren Albers, likes to reflect when things turn out differently than she'd planned but within the scope of her own intentions that, "There are no wrong turns." Interestingly, contentment has a fundamental belief that all directions taken on every path, when paved with your personally defined intentions, will ultimately lead to a door that looks like home.

A Story of Calm Intention

One of the greatest assets of being clear on my intentions is the sense of calm I can experience, even in the midst of remarkable chaos or even risk. What do I mean by calm? Here's a story to explain.

"How do I begin to explain how calm is something that she—"

"Just remind her."

"She *asked* for it as a gift. A gift! What am I supposed to do—tell her she's asking for something that she's already got?"

"Yes. *That's* the real gift. Telling her. Go on. Go—tell her!"

It was just a short walk to her table.

"Hey. Um. You know that feeling you get when snow blankets everything inches deep, and it's untrodden. and sound is both muffled and heightened? And you let go of all your busy plans because no one, not even you, is going anywhere. For quite a while. *That* feeling? You know it?"

"Yes," she did know it.

"Well, that's calm. Really, it is. You know those last moments before the huge event you've planned for months, those moments when everything has finally come together and you know, even though your mind is racing and you're wondering if you've remembered everything? That moment when you realize that if you have forgotten something, it's too late to do anything about it now, and you just move on ahead and press the GO button?'

"Yep, I've been there."

"That's calm." Relieved that she looked like she understood, he finished making his point.

"People mistake mellowness for calm. Calm isn't always mellow. In fact, sometimes it can look and be frenetic. Calm is that assurance an astronaut feels after years of preparation, just before blast-off. It's when you've done your best, you've done all you can do, and you are ready to step on stage. Calm is the one who starts every show."

Chapter 1

Live with Intention

*"Set the intention to pay attention.
Magic will happen."*

—Bo Mackison

Setting an intention: it's a big part of what I teach, and it never fails to result in magic. For years, I've been facilitating an online workshop that is all about paying attention to the ordinary happenings in life and then discovering the extraordinary in the everyday. I suggest that the folks in my group take photos of "yellow," and they respond "Wow, never knew there was so much yellow in my day! Amazing!" And then suddenly, they are paying attention to much more than just yellow objects. They begin to delight in the small wonders of their ordinary everyday lives.

I ask the group members to hold a question gently in their minds, no forcing, no big research. Simply set the intention to pay attention, then notice what happens. One mid-level finance executive asked, "How do I find time in a life run by schedules to do fun art projects?" Give the question time and space to percolate. Your brain is hardwired for internal brainstorming! Your brain will get busy and start creating answers—if you listen without judgment. (I always encourage keeping note-taking materials in a handy pocket, for answers will pop up at the most unexpected times.) The executive listened to her wise inner voice and then followed through with the idea that most spoke to her: she assembled a pencil-case sized art kit filled with the needed supplies to create small mandalas. Now she creates in those in-between moments that might have once been overlooked.

Setting intentions doesn't have to be about life-altering decisions—though they can be. Sometimes the smallest of intentions do indeed have life-altering consequences. I always encourage participants in my classes to "set the intention to pay attention." And then I add this promise, which has yet to fail: "Magic will happen."

—Bo Mackison

Your Day Has a Soundtrack

Your intentions are essentially the soundtrack of your day. That soundtrack plays under everything you do. They are the poetry written into the pauses of your experience. They are the breathtaking colors of your dawn; they cover the paths you walk and pave the roads you drive. Defined or undefined, your intentions are the light that makes seeing your path possible. Both practical and practice-able, the intentions you hold define both your days and, ultimately, your life. It is evident why knowing with specificity what they are and how they work in your daily life can enhance everything you undertake.

***

When the press of the world and the challenges inherent in any life threaten to overwhelm, your intentions press back. Rather than accepting the requirements of external systems as a matter of course, you are able to embrace what is genuinely true and applicable for you. Would you know what you believe? Watch how you live. Do you wonder what really matters to you? Listen to the stories that you consistently tell others. Listen to the internal voice that you allow to narrate what is happening in the world around you. Pay attention to the memories that come unbidden and play on repeat in your mind. Observe the patterns that you lay down with your actions, and notice the words that you use with yourself and those in your immediate circle of influence. How do you finish out your day? What is the manner in which you greet your morning, and how do you establish your plan and your path for the minutes in front of you? These are all indicators of the intentions that you bring to your life. They are the ways that you begin to see how your fundamental intentions are manifesting in the course of your way. Do you like what you see? Reinforce it. Are you less than happy with what you observe? You have the power to give yourself fresh direction.

Who's in That Mirror?

*"Friendship with oneself is all-important,
because without it one cannot be friends
with anyone else in the world."*

—Eleanor Roosevelt

Eleanor Roosevelt knew a lot about keeping her own counsel.
She understood that in a world that was critical of her voice, her
height, her political views, and her relationships, she had to extend
acceptance and kindness to herself—first. She knew she would not
always be able to depend on it from others. Essentially, she knew that
she was teaching others how to treat her by the manner in which she
treated and befriended herself. There's plenty of conversation about
the accountability that is required from one person: the one you see
when you look in the mirror. Your own assessments of your life have
the greatest significance and impact. It may be tempting to live a
life that is pleasing to others, but if you live a life that is not pleasing
to you, what resources do you have to call upon? The appraisal of
others has power or influence over you—if you permit it. I can value
your opinion without it compelling me to change a position. I can
acknowledge your judgment without allowing myself to be either
deterred or determined by it. I echo Eleanor's sentiments and aspire
to love myself in order to fully love others. Certainly this means my
way of living my own intentions does not have to meet the approval
of anyone else. Or perhaps, it must first meet my own approval before
I might care to observe if anyone else approves.

A Case for Writing

There are many things in a day that will capture your attention, but only a few will resonate with the aspirations of your intentions. Pay attention to the ones that do. I encourage you to write—to have the courage to pick up an instrument and correspond with yourself. At your keyboard, compose a very personal letter describing the surprising discoveries or evident patterns in your day. I want you to write because you know so much more than you think you know. If you are already inclined toward a personal writing practice, you know the richness of inquiry and discovery that waits on those pages. If you have not yet enjoyed the benefits of writing your observations, say along with a very impressive collection of humans what Flannery O'Connor admitted: "I write to discover what I know."

***

If you are willing to be both teacher and student, you will teach yourself to focus and learn to observe the details of your day. That observation allows you to enrich what works well for you and identify the things, activities, and people that do not align with or support your intentions. In this willingness to observe, you find that everywhere is a classroom and every moment is an opportunity to grow further into your truest self. Let your heart inform your eyes. Follow your intentions as if you were a raven and the choices in alignment and of consequence were all the sparkling, shiny bits that capture your attention. When you are mindfully aware of the relationship that your intentions have to your actions, you are able to more readily recognize those moments when you are in flow and the other times when something feels out of kilter. In the process of writing about what you see in your own experiences, you are creating a field of understanding which aligns more cohesively with your intentions.

***

I taught a writing course in a medium security prison for almost five years. I entered by undergoing a strenuous security check each time. I was aware of the weight of the metal gates as they shut behind me, portal after portal. Yet, restrained behind those barriers, gates, and walls, I saw certain proof of the freedom that writing brings. Some of the participants were looking at a life sentence without hope of parole. Others were counting the weeks or months until their release date. At the start of every one of the dozens of classes I taught, I noticed a single commonality. Many of these incarcerated individuals were not connected to their motivations for past actions, nor were they clear on what their intentions were. They had goals to stay legal, stay clear, show up for their families on the outside...but intentions? When I initially asked what their intentions were, the answers were the same. The common answer was, "I don't know." Being unaware or unclear of your intentions for your life allows the random winds of whim to govern your step. Certainly I am not suggesting that absent knowledge of your intention, you are destined for a life of criminal activity. The writing practices that these individuals pursued allowed them to understand the difference between a goal and an intention. They crafted and formalized personal manifestos. I learned that over time, doing so made a significant difference for many of those imprisoned. They may have been physically behind a wall, but how they chose to consider each day before them slowly set them free. Writing can do that.

Invest in Consistent Measure

Goldilocks teaches a lot about evaluating with consistent measures. Too hot. Too cold. Just right. Just right is the bandwidth that underscores everything that is identified by ease and satisfaction... "Ahhhhh, just right" is a response to a thing that fits itself, perfectly.

It's a wireless signal with full bars. It's a vintage analog radio tuned with precision to a broadcast. When I invest the time in mindfulness of my own day and activities, I benefit from the conscious, objective (as objective as I can be about myself) observation by looking at the "too" in my events and decisions. Too much. Too little. Too general. Too controlling. The "too" assessment isn't just for qualitative review. Easy familiarity with your intentions becomes a quick litmus for everything you touch, do, or consider. It can be one of the primary considerations for most decisions you make. Here's a practical model for you to consider as I'm talking about measures.

> **Impact:** Does it align with my intentions?
> **Improve:** Does it improve the manner in which my intentions are articulated?
> **Increase:** Does it add value or increase the effectiveness of my intentions?

One Thing and Many Things

I share this Rumi reference again: "If we do everything else but that one thing, we will be lost. And if we do nothing else but that one thing, we will have lived a glorious life."

Inspired by Rumi's reference to The One Thing, I call my intentions, collectively, my one thing. They are many things synergistically coming together—a braid, of sorts, essentially a lifeline of focus and clarity bringing personal contentment and peace in a chaotic world. Chosen elements weave together to create a state, a mindset of growth, learning, and purposefulness called intentional living. An ancient saying asserts,

> *outside the tent, chaos.*
> *inside the tent, peace.*

Living a big, openhearted life can be messy. Living in such a way as to detach from expectation and still manage to live with intention creates a peaceful orderliness of the spirit. Spirit: inside your own tent. To be in that space is to remain unruffled in the face of a flurry; to dance through a storm, unharmed; to duck and pivot with grace of movement while punches are being thrown; to remain centered and present to a friend who is experiencing the crisis of loss. These are all opportunities for the alchemy that occurs when you live aligned with your intentions. Everyone's mechanism for understanding their own intentions is unique to them. What one person weaves together to craft an intentional way of directing the route of their life is different from that of another… It's not the prescriptive practice that matters (even the one that I offer you in this book) as much as the predictable outcome—that of specifically knowing what your intentions are and understanding how they guide and direct you in virtually every action you take. Your intentions are the witness, the affirmation that you are living authentically.

Old Road

I know in my bones
when I first strike foot to stone.
This road has a storied way.
The old road has seen patriots
call for independence, footfalls
turn over to
horses, give way to
carriages and
wooden wheels
to tires.
It has held the rushes and clatter
of ill ones being hurried to care
and of those betrothed heading
to their lifetime of together.

All the while stone silently
observing the progression.
I know it in my bones
when I tread this
tried and tired earth
that it is my beautiful witness
quietly holding
space for me to
notice.
And bow.
And thank the trees.

Chapter 2

Completion
Walk to the Edge

"A dream begins with an idea."

—Linda Bannan

As I toss that potential around in my mind, the essential process begins to take shape. The supply list forms, the excitement builds, and next steps fall into place. The idea becomes a project as I accomplish and celebrate each step. At some point, enthusiasm wanes, the project falters, and I begin to plod slowly. Remembering the excitement of that initial spark of the idea restores momentum. I figure out the next steps and continue steadfast movement toward completion, knowing that…

With completion, the dream comes true!

A few years ago, while strolling along a white sugar sand beach, I was wishing I could take the beach and its memories home with me so I could breathe in and enjoy being there any time. I began to gather bits of shells, drifted wood, and pockmarked rocks, taking care to gather the imperfect rather than searching for perfect shells, wood, and rocks. I wanted the real beach, not an idealized one.

I started with a small piece of indigo-dyed fabric because it looked like water meeting sand. First, I handstitched where the blue fabric turned white to emphasize the waves' edges. Next, I arranged and rearranged the beach bits I'd gathered. Once I settled on a design that felt right, I stitched some of those bits onto the fabric. Soon after, my beach time ended; I flew home and daily life resumed. I didn't even think about my beach art project until two years later!

After the rediscovery, I stitched on the remaining beach remnants, then puzzled over how to complete it. The last steps in creating an art quilt are adding a back, binding, and sleeve from which to hang it, but I didn't think this work was ready for those final steps yet. It needed something more—another texture, a pop of color, something. Then I spotted a piece of gold-dyed cheesecloth on my worktable and knew I'd figured it out. Again, I arranged and rearranged until all the pieces looked (and felt) right. As I stitched those netlike fibers onto this piece, the title came to me, and *A Day at the Beach* was ready for completion. She now hangs in my studio and takes me to that white sugar sand beach every day!

—Linda Bannan

Just Begin It

My skill set is not a rigid, contained metal box of tools but rather a glowing, expanding, contracting, breathing well of alchemical abilities that expand with my willingness to learn, breathe more deeply, and dig into any size task. I take advantage of my ability to see how a large thing is constructed of many small things. I allow myself the thrill and freedom of completing one small thing in the context of the large. That's what I mean by "just begin it." Considering the whole of a massive project is overwhelming. Even on ordinary days, there is often more DO than DOne. Working in small bits toward a larger completion ultimately gets it all done.

***

I was thirteen when my mother died of a heart attack. My father worked the graveyard shift at a manufacturing plant. It was in this unanticipated circumstance that I learned to ask myself, "If I knew how this worked, what's the first thing I would do?" I'd speculate an answer, and then I would do that thing. This inquiry became, "How would I act if I pretended this was easy?" These were significant questions as I navigated my life without any immediate adult supervision. As I learned how to cook, I recognized a significant, transferrable skill in the process of following a recipe. First, one is advised to gather all of the ingredients so as to avoid discovery halfway through that one essential ingredient is missing. This is a template for any kind of beginning. Just as Linda Bannan references gathering elements for her artwork, you collect the things you imagine you will need: materials, resources, the support of others—

whatever you imagine. Some of the stuff will end up being unused. And other needs will arise that you did not anticipate. That's how it goes. The first and sometimes most difficult aspect to amazing, creative productivity (or a creative edge of any kind) is in this initial action: gather what you suppose you will need and begin.

***

Ideas and opportunities and that ever-present list of "to do" occasionally feel like the flock in that classic Hitchcock horror film, *The Birds*: menacing, dangerous, and threatening to land on your head at any moment. The vision of completion scatters those birds like a powerful gust of wind and leaves just one. One bird…one bird is not so scary. One creative idea. One small task. Then all that remains is to begin it. No repeated procrastinating. No excuses and no anxiety. Pablo Picasso made an inquiry that's made a lifelong impression on me. He wondered if an artist knew in advance exactly how and what they were going to create, why would they even bother creating it? Much of the pleasure of beginning and continuing onward to the next right task lies in the pleasure of discovery. Task by task the journey takes you to completion.

Begin as If You Intend to Finish

So often procrastination whispers in your ear that if you are unable to imagine what it will look like, precisely, when you are done, how will you know if you have done it right? Anxiety begs you to wait until you are certain you have every single thing you could possibly need. The courage to begin is modeled in so many things we do every day. It's tempting to say that you do not know how to begin a big thing, much less complete it. In fact, if you wake to the day and get out of bed, you model beginning things all day long!

These are some ways to begin a thing—beginning a thing without knowing how it might end.

See a friend. Walk in a garden. Take a deep breath. Try something new. Go a new way. Find out the name of a tree in your neighborhood. Plant a tree if there isn't one. Greet a stranger. Plant seeds. Watch the weather. Wait. Believe. Make a gift for a friend or a stranger. Post a card. Give a smile. Offer to help. Appreciate a soldier. Play with a puppy. Stand in the wind. Walk up a hill. Stretch. Wonder. Imagine. Clean your closet. Use a different colored pen. Use crayons. Dance. Sing a little song. Do the unexpected. Be extraordinary. Say yes to most things. Pretend it's easy. Say you're sorry. Use a new spice. Laugh loudest. Write something. Be original. Be well. Practice. Hop. Skip. Jump. Kiss somebody. Be special. Imagine something. Tell a story. Listen. Inspire. Be inspired. Swell with pride. Brag. Rearrange. Go somewhere for no particular reason and see what you learn. Eat an apple. Be grateful. Go ahead and weep for this never-to-be-seen-again moment. Love as deeply as you can.

***

In many of these familiar actions you see the skill of choosing to begin. You may say that you do not know how to start a thing…but your personal lesson plan is written in the hundreds, if not tens of thousands, of things that you have already started and completed.

The point is clear: just begin the thing. And begin it with completion, the edge, the finish in mind. It doesn't mean that what you imagine is where you'll end up. But it gives you the capacity to head at least in the general direction of where you want to end up. Beginning a thing certainly does not mean that you will finish it any time close to now. But one thing is certain: if you do not begin, you will not finish. Not ever. I've noticed that unbegun and unfinished things both have very loud voices.

March along! Sing your song as you learn your way through the next right task of anything, big or small. Sing quietly or sing at the top of your lungs. If you make certain to have a little fun along the way, it's more likely that you will continue along the way to closing out the project. Don't succumb to the tyranny of immediacy. Just do what you can, when you can, and recognize that, on many days, the assessment of "pretty darn good" ranks right up there close to "practically perfect." Look in the mirror and remind yourself of how amazing and accomplished you are. While you are looking, remind yourself also that a successive series of starts will put you that much closer to the finish.

***

Does it seem contradictory that I address completion in the context of intention? Does it somehow blur the line between an intention and a goal? Perhaps, yes. I am reconciled to the presence of many contradictions in the manner by which I am able to embrace my days. If you are not, maybe this idea will help. Walking to an edge can be living to the edge of your capacity. It can mean envisioning not one way of pursuing your way, but many ways. To walk to the edge is to ask so much of yourself.

Call Them Targeted Completion Dates

Deadline. Dead. Line. Just mouthing the words sounds ominous. The history of this word claims 1864 as its first appearance in the written record. Fascinated by the resistance I experienced toward this word, I researched its origin some years ago. What I learned produced a language change that I employ to this day. During the American Civil War, prisoners were seldom held in purpose-built jails. Troop movements were unpredictable, and rarely did they billet or quarter themselves more than a few days at a time. As a consequence, prisoners were herded into open spaces and made to stay within makeshift boundaries. Those confines had two lines, generally defined by branches laid end to end. A prisoner who stepped over the inner boundary line was verbally ordered back. A prisoner who disregarded the warning and stepped over the second line was shot. They were not shot to warn or wound, but to kill. That's the provenance of the word we use broadly today, deadline.

***

In my own quest for completion of practically anything, I've determined to no longer use the term "deadline." I call them "targeted completion dates." Unless there will truly be life-impacting consequences if the project is not completed on a specific date, I do not contribute to any inevitable anxiety that surrounds keeping a time-specific commitment. More reflective of the truth of my life is a targeted completion date. I aim to reach my targets! Yes, I do. If my aim misses? I reset the target (negotiate or renegotiate) and aim again. In some cases, I've been known to declare, "Close enough," and carry on with the next right thing. And so far, I'm alive to tell the tale!

The Long-Term Done Lives in Today's DO

> "Love is the only force capable of transforming an enemy to a friend."
>
> —Dr. Martin Luther King, Jr.

I spent a day focused on these words of Dr. King. Throughout my day, these words challenged me to love the many drivers I encountered who were behaving badly. One car had parked itself in the drive lane. The passenger was obviously taking down information from a "for rent" sign. I cautiously drove around them instead of honking or shaking a shaming finger. Dr. King's admonishing phrase kept my road responses rooted in love instead of harshness. This single focus impacts my mindfulness while driving to this day.

***

How about taxes? The IRS. Yes. It would be tempting, even easy, to consider the predictable requirement of taxes as an enemy of sorts. Often, through the phenomenon of procrastination, the filing of annual taxes becomes a looming "targeted completion date," one that can have substantial consequences if not completed within a prescribed time. I have spent years building an undesirable habit—the habit of deferring this task. In the context of Dr. King's words, I wondered how the force to which he referred might transform my experience. Would the force of love actually work with preparing taxes? I asked myself a question: if it was something I really enjoyed doing, how would I treat it? Then I applied that answer to this task. I created an inviting working environment near windows with lots of light and a lovely view. I added two tables so I had plenty of space to organize and not feel closed in. I set out my favorite paper and my best pens. I put on my favorite music. And whoooosh, I began to experiment in this context with Dr. King's words.

In this reframing effort, I am an artist in the land of figures, numbers, and columns. I thought about the professionals who spend all of their working days in these ways. While pursuing this endeavor that I had consistently treated like an enemy, I decided to express gratitude for the industry and be thankful that there are professionals who find ease and reward in tasks I typically resist. I enjoyed making my notes and recording in lovely form. I used all of the things that I know I enjoy in other activities to make this one feel more welcoming. I celebrated each category that I finished. I make sure to hydrate and nourish myself in the course of the effort. I chose to focus on the

services and advantages that my tax dollars deliver to me as a citizen:
services, roads, postal delivery, water treatment plants, public parks,
libraries! I *love* libraries. My momentum only increased as I practiced
applying successful approaches from other activities in this unlikely
scenario. I did walk to the edge of my process—and I completed
those taxes. And I did so without the typical companion of dread
and resentment.

This task, one that had previously been onerous in its completion, was
transformed because I transferred certain things that I knew I enjoyed
into the process and topped them off with a commitment toward love.
With a shift in perspective and a focus on a single phrase, I completed
the thing. The DO arrived at DOne with a lot less anxiety. At the
end of the matter, I felt changed in a measurable way, one that was
personal and practical. Dr. King understood that love is the prime
place where transformation intersects with our perspective.

Speak Quietly to Yourself

Speak quietly to yourself and promise that there will be better days.

Allow the unfinished tasks to make their noise and whisper a quiet
assurance to yourself that you will continue with your best effort.
Console your tender spirit with reminders and models of other
successes. Take comfort in practical ways of the kinds that you would
offer your finest friend. Recognize that, on certain days, the greatest
grace is to let the undone remain undone for one more day, and you
get to close your eyes.

Chapter 3

Spirit
Listen Hard

*"I create art in order to discover
the divinity within myself."*

—Pat Wiederspan Jones

For many years, I have been creating little boxes with found objects assembled inside them. I love collecting little "treasures" that hold meaning to me. These sacred objects include things like feathers, buttons that look like the shiny moon, seashells, small figurines of goddesses, a Mona Lisa, circles of all kinds, sticks, birds, and on and on. Natural objects and anything else, and little figures of the Virgin Mary, in all her appearances. Rusty bottle caps can become halos. Vintage silk roses nestle at Mary's feet. Stars shine above her head. These assemblages have found homes in boxes, frames, tins, tiny cathedrals, and even sardine tins. They have become shrines, but to what? For the longest time, I did not understand why I was making these or what they were all about. I only knew they were important to me.

One day I found myself standing in front of an exhibit of these works with a friend, trying to explain to him what they were about. In talking with him, I learned that every little thing that I chose to insert into these assemblages symbolized something sacred to me. Art is expressed through symbols, and I was using symbols. I was listening to my soul in each of these choices. And finally, in listening to my own words, listening hard as I chose my words, I realized that I was creating these works in an effort to find the divinity within myself. I was searching for the Divine Feminine, with the shells and images of the moon, nature, the goddess, and Mary. Now, by listening more intently to my own spirit and intuition, I have a new understanding that I am also a divine being.

—Pat Wiederspan Jones

In Listening to Others, I Can Hear the Universe

*"It was Johann Wolfgang von Goethe who said,
"A person hears only what they understand."*

A familiar refrain begins many arguments. "But I told you…"

"You did not."

"Yes! I did. Three times."

"You did?"

"Yes. I explained it to you three different times."

"I must not have heard you."

"You heard me, all right. Apparently, you just didn't understand. Why didn't you tell me you didn't understand instead of just nodding your head?"

Sound familiar? It's a good question, really. Goethe was clear. We readily hear what we already understand. It's hard to tell someone when I do not understand, because in the moment, I'm not exactly certain if I do or don't. It's erroneously said that you can't teach an old dog new tricks. The first and only trick a dog of any age needs to learn or know is how to listen. Listen hard and well, and, in concert with that listening, learn how to effectively communicate in response.

I've seen Goethe's words at play in so many ways. You may recall that when cartoonist Charles Schultz had any adult speak in his imagined *Peanuts* world, we never really knew what the adult was saying. It was only represented as a series of repetitive sounds, "Mwah. Mwah. Mwah."

Focusing on this observation from Goethe allowed me to observe the number of times in a day when I can hear words spoken without being able to understand what they mean. Even though I have developed several different habits over the years to help me be a better listener, I still have the experience of not understanding what is being said. Often, I will simply confess that I am unclear. Sometimes I am able to say, "Would you please say that to me in another way?" These responses have allowed me to inform myself that I was not grasping a message and have given me a second opportunity to understand.

In learning to listen hard and invite new patterns into my old ways, I lean against the wall of uncertainty and am able to whisper, "This one thing I know for certain…I want to understand." In that longing for understanding, it's easy to assume that one is only considering the function of the ears. To listen hard involves more than a single organ. A person absent the capacity to hear understands that the skill of listening requires other senses besides auditory capacity. One must also look and empathize in order to listen hard. Hearing. Seeing. Feeling. They make an effective partnership. Being willing to see, hear, and experience the best in others, some would say being willing to see the divine in others, transforms experience.

***

I consider the intention to listen hard to be the most spiritual of these intentions I adopt. It's a compulsion that extends beyond human relationship. Listening, being deeply aware of intuition, of cosmic nudges, of serendipities so remarkable that it's easy to believe they are divine, these are all elements involved in the impulse to listen hard. So many times I have chastised myself, saying, "I *knew* it! That was my first impulse and I disregarded it." Essentially, I can listen and hear that whisper from my own soul, yet there are all kinds of reasons that I choose to ignore it. When I thoughtfully consider a raft of options and make sure that tending my intuition is among those options, I usually make a better decision. Listening hard to that inner impulse, that sense of spiritual or internal guidance, is often cited as a key factor in successful endeavors. Perhaps you can think of someone you know or a person of note who has gone against general consensus, following their own counsel, and for whom the consequence for that trust, that listening, has been extraordinary. Perhaps you can think of times that it has happened for you. Listen hard.

It is rightly said that we see what we are looking for and tend to hear what we expect to be said. In this heightened sense of listening, it is possible to hear more accurately, to see more clearly. On days when I actively practice listening hard, I not only feel more connected to others, I experience a more significant connection to myself. Being willing to experience the best that others have to offer lifts a curtain. Old stories are left behind, and we have the capacity to hear the truth in an action—to see it for what it actually is. This leans toward seeing greater beauty; we can see through facade and notice that which serves as a warning. Maya Angelou famously admonished people to believe what a person first shows you about who they are. It's tempting to not listen to those first whispers of warning. There are people in the world who intend to bring harm. And it's tempting to overwrite what you hear and see with a story that suits you better than what you are hearing. This is another case for listening hard. Harm and hardship can be turned away at the door if I can learn to listen hard to my instinct and believe what I hear, see, and feel.

Seen OR Unseen, a World Exists Beside Me

In the realm of Spirit, there is a synergy beyond hearing or seeing to consider God. The idea of God/God-ness, or for those uncomfortable with the subject, GOoDness or GOoD, is not containable. It is indefinable—unrestrainable. The moment someone declares, "THIS. Aha. THIS is God, or God is this," GOoD will appear as something undeclared and unexpected. Beyond the immediate grasp of human thought, GOoD is the ultimate magic show of the universe. I write this with levels of trepidation because so many people rely on alignment and agreement with others in order to accept one's view of GOoD. Even adding that "o" could ruffle some feathers among those reading this. This is the nature of listening hard...recognizing that the opinions of others need not align with your own in order to be valid. There is so much about the nature of Spirit, of Universal GoODness, that is held in the hands of opinion. There are so many names for this force. And my understanding is limited, which is why I ask of myself to listen as hard as I can and be aware that the world in which I stand is likely not the only world that exists. There are so many different names for the force that many call GOoD. I hear it and see it in joy, in sorrow, in pain, in understanding, in perplexity, in how we rise up and in the manner we fall down, in how we can see our reflection and in how we cannot conceive of how we are or how the world is, when things seem in order and when things appear chaotic—in all these walks and ways, we can know there is a universal force that supports our breath. In spite of anything and because of everything, we know. And we must remember to listen. That universal force isn't always sweet and considerate. The still small voice prefers not to rise to crescendo in order to be heard. Of course, sometimes it appears to resort to some whoop-ass, but only when listening hard is absent from the exchange. This really is a case for paying attention!

Pay Attention

Pay attention to the synchronicity of the events in your life. People have different names for those visiting signals, the signs, the synergies of our lives. I had a unique understanding of God when I was very young. It often amused my Sunday School teachers, and it got me in conflict with some of the adults in the small world that was the church around the corner from my home. I remember with fondness conceptual arm-wrestling matches of ideas with a cherished cousin who was a biblical scholar. I remember one holiday when we were sent to the kitchen, behind a door, because our discourse, which we found fascinating, was too loud and making some uncomfortable. My cousin took exception to my saying that my coming to know God was a magic carpet ride. But he understood the sense of wonder, he listened to the awe that the reference implied. In that awe, I said yes to GOoD and GOoDness and have been saying yes ever since. He demonstrated the capacity to rise above the language of his embraced doctrine and see and hear me. Because he allowed that, I did not have to speak of matters of faith in the same way he did. We were able to take different roads and meet at the same door. Listening hard makes that kind of compassionate understanding possible.

Learn to Listen with a Practiced Pause

Racers at the starting line are poised, positioned to surge forward at the sound of the starting gun. There are some conversations that unfold like that: so excited about a thought, or a point to be made, or a resonant experience to share, I stop listening and start looking for the opportunity to speak. The first perceptible pause in the other person's statements become the starting gun. I jump. Start. Seize the single opportunity to get my sentences in. But have I listened? No. And with this kind of rush to speak, on one or both parts, is it really a conversation or is it more like a dragrace with words?

When I really listen hard, I take notes. If paper and pen are not available, I attempt to replicate ideas with mental notes. I find taking actual notes far more effective. There's a lot of support for the benefit of such note taking. It heightens accurate recollection of what was said. It also assists in making the information available for quick recall.

In an effort to be a good listener, I often write down something I want to remember to contribute while allowing the person who is speaking to conclude uninterrupted. When I take notes, I speak less. When I pause my talking habit and really focus on what the other person is saying, I am more likely to ask questions than to make statements. It becomes less a game of my turn, now your turn, and more a collaborative effort to create something greater than our individual thoughts and experiences. It's a little like cooperatively preparing a meal in a kitchen, the results of which will nourish both chefs and anyone else who happens to be near the table.

There are many different ways to listen and things to listen to. It is said that music is made as much of the silences between the notes as of the notes themselves. So it must be in this process of learning to listen hard. The spaces in between, the practiced pause, contribute in a profound way to the learning that occurs when listening is present. Do we listen to "spirit" any differently than we listen to our friends? It's possible that it is all a matter of continual practice and that each mode—hearing, seeing, and feeling—informs the other. Memory, intuition, and experience can all play into listening hard. It takes practice to learn the pause—to be in that space between the notes.

Origami as Metaphor for Listening Hard

The patterns, the visual unlikelihood, the stretching of one's imagination as it asks, "A flat piece of paper did that?" The interconnectedness of the origami folds strikes me as symbolic of the complex layers and folds of our days. Crease, fold, severe straight lines, each flat fold building upon flat fold until shaken or the strength of a breath is applied. With breath or stretch, there is transformation. Another form is recognized. What was familiar in one iteration becomes a bird in flight, a box, or a flower. This brings to mind those *aha* moments—when all the murky, disconnected complexities line up in magnificent order to say, "Here. Listen and look. This is the lesson I have been creating for you. Here is this lasting, difficult beauty for your life." Just as with origami, this kind of listening takes practice.

***

In learning to listen, we must be both gentle and fierce. We must be willing to see beyond what we expect and courageous enough to honestly hear what is being said and to believe what is being demonstrated.

Currency of Spirit

The important words of your soul are your currency.

These are the words that make marks, that write on the pages of your days, that authorize expenditures and deposits in the bank account of your heart.

These words are your currency, your investment, your capitalization of endeavor.

Yes, deposit them in the bank account of your heart, paint them on your soul, write them on your hand, wear them like jewelry. Let them lead what you teach and say; let them be the spice in your food and the exclamations in your conversations. May these good words of yours be the road you walk, the light of dawn that greets you, and the lullaby that sends you to peaceful, restorative sleep. May these words be strengthened by the wrap and reinforcement of your intentions.

Chapter 4

Health
Practice Wellness

"Wellness fuels my vision."

"I never understood that success didn't bring my best life until I had to make changes just to live."

—Kim Jayhan

I almost died four years ago. My doctor said, "There must be a reason you survived. No more working. Go live your best life."

Devastated that my career had abruptly ended, I contemplated my life. I had enjoyed a wonderful family and a loving partner relationship. An executive job gave me financial security. I was a recognized health analytics expert, national speaker, and writer. I had received accolades from my employer and clients. Isn't that living your best life?

Turns out, no. I worked sixty to seventy-five hours a week, with heavy travel and little sleep, even working on vacation to meet deadlines. I literally fell asleep sitting in my chair at the Thanksgiving dinner table. Self-care? No, my needs were always last. I had no time to practice wellness.

***

Time to change and live with intention. Getting proper sleep most nights gave me the best start each day. I dreamt more, created more. Eating right gave my body the energy needed to create and my mind the energy needed to imagine.

An art journal was my opportunity to try new techniques. I collected ideas as though I was capturing twinkly fireflies for my own special inspiration jar. I savored time with family, friends, and pets. I traveled less, but when I did, I enjoyed myself. Conversations with my grandchildren propelled my creativity. I read more books. I created a vision for myself. I released my first children's book and opened a publishing company.

Now, my healthcare analytics are focused on me and my bliss. I wake each day excited to focus on my dreams. My wellness fuels my vision, so I don't shortcut routines. Quiet time provides the ability to define and prioritize my lists. I drink more water and tea, less coffee. I eat healthier food. I listen to music more, and, each quarter, I evaluate my creative goals. I'm more present with those in my life. Doing what I love and living with intention has brought joy, peace, and happiness to my life. Now, this is my best life.

—Kim Jayhan

Self-Care: Movement toward Health

"Chop wood, carry water." It's a time honored zen saying. The context is that whether you are an enlightened being or not, there are still basic actions that you need to complete on any given day. Many business leaders like to talk about the action of cutting your own wood warming you more than once—in the exercise itself and then in the fire it fuels. Though the obvious connection to wellness is seen in the cardiovascular benefit of such action, I perceive the meaning to be: take care of yourself first by tending the fundamental requirements of your environment. Many consider altruism the hallmark of an elevated soul. Giving primary care to yourself first is not only practical, it is also essential. Individuals trained in the liturgy of self-sacrifice and denial have difficulty seeing the balance between self-care and self-indulgence. With objective consideration, they appear quite different. And they actually *are* quite different.

***

Self-care tends to the fundamental requirements of a healthy and contented life. A healthy person will choose the comfort and ease of another person above their own, periodically but not constantly. If daily bread is a metaphor for all essentials, then if you feed your whole baguette to someone with great frequency, you become a need for someone else to fill. The factor of generosity, so rewarding in a healthy lifestyle, can become self-indulgence. The conventional grasp of this phrase involves giving too much to others. So how is giving to others self-indulgent? Generosity turned to indulgently giving too much, to over-giving to the detriment of your own values and needs, becomes a type of martyrdom: "I've given so much. How could they treat me this way? I've given everything I had. I'm all poured out." Go ahead and ask yourself, "Who is doing the pouring and why?"

***

Providing your own essential needs empowers you to care not only for yourself, but for others. Tending watchfully to your requirements builds a resource base that allows for positive generosity. Generosity and (re)generative share a Latin root meaning, among other things, "magnanimous" or "to create." Regenerating is restoring what was spent. Generating is the process of creating what previously did not exist. As a generous soul, I grasp the impulse to "give it all away." Consider a sourdough baguette. Sourdough starter generously recreates itself only as long as some portion is retained and intentionally fed additional flour and water.

In Perspective: Choices Are Opportunities

Perspective's a funny thing. As challenging as my own experience may seem, there is always someone "who's got it worse than I do." Here's what I know: "There are starving children in Ethiopia" did nothing to help me eat the ubiquitous tomato aspic that found its way to a waiting, trembling platter of iceberg lettuce at so many of my childhood meals. I was willing to send as much of that aspic to those hungry children as I might pack. But from my limited understanding of the postal system and relative worldwide distances, I just wasn't sure that aspic would travel all that well.

My point?

Comparison of our own pain to the pain of others is an ineffective tool. My pain is my pain—period. The pain is not lessened by recognizing that someone else's pain seems more complex than mine. I find that such comparisons only invite my inner drillmaster to appear and start barking at me, "C'mon along, wimpy little soldier, there are others who bear up so much better than you!"

***

Comparison simply serves as an override button to disregard my own best interests and plough through the pain. That's what almost did me in one spring. When I got bronchitis, I told myself that it wasn't as bad as last year. Then it moved into pneumonia, and I said that I didn't feel as poorly as I imagined one would feel with pneumonia. "It's not that bad." You've done it? Fill in your own blank: "It's not as bad as ____ (insert your own appropriate, relevant kind of comparison). Rubbish, I say. It's all just dressed-up denial—denial masquerading as noble suffering and inappropriate overextending. I should have compassion—for all. Hear me speak in my best five-year-old voice, "Me first." Yes, indeed. Compassionate care for ourselves needs a higher rank in our days. It is an ongoing life lesson for me to grasp that my profound service to others must first begin with service to myself. May I have the fortitude to see and serve my own needs first, this very day, that I might fully and uncompromisingly fulfill my vision of service to others. In fact, to greet the day in this way:

Dear Day: I greet you with ease and rising wellness. I invite you to shepherd the right people into all my spaces. In all my ventures, let me be reminded that they are first spiritual adventures before they are any other kind of venture. In all your elements, I am both a willing student and teacher. I am content to be both magician and muse. I embrace each choice as an opportunity to measure the action against my own intentions. I anticipate a consistent energy on all your paths and at your end, I suspect sleep will come upon me sweetly. Glad you're here,

Love,
—Me

Honoring the Health of Others

Health and wellness are two essential things that are most noted in their absence. My friend Kathleen often reminds me that it's best to reward the behavior you would like to see repeated. Can you think of a time at a restaurant when somebody at the table made fun of the person who ordered the "heart healthy" option or opted for a salad rather than a three-course meal—as if somehow, the healthy choice they were making for themselves was intended as a buzzkill or an indictment of the choice that they were making? How about reframing that to celebrate the focus on health? You might even consider being inspired by the break from convention or expectation. I have a friend who has chosen a sober lifestyle for the sake of her health and her personal productivity and happiness. Just the other day she commented how challenging social situations are for her. Her non-imbibing is seen as an affront to those who have a drink in their hand…or their second…or their fifth. They are called "personal choices" for a reason. There are good times to not take someone else's actions personally—and making healthy choices based upon a very individual metric are among those times.

***

I don't wear a lot of pink. I don't have a contentious relationship with the color pink—it's just not one of my favorites. However, I've worn pink and made art with pink quite a lot for a friend of mine named Roxanne.

I wear pink as often as I'm asked because of her. She lived to make the choice to wear pink any old time she pleases. She survived to earn the right to show this pink ribbon while she walks for a cause—for a cure. She walks to honor all her peers who have survived to thrive; she walks to remember those who have ended their journey; she walks to encourage those who are still learning from the taskmaster commonly called breast cancer.

She walks, and I wear pink without commentary on the organizations who use pink ribbons in their marketing and without judgement on all the ways pink is exploited to mean singularly female. Because when she wears and uses pink, it is less a marketing thing—less a political statement—and more a declaration that she survived a very hard thing, so she walks and wears that color to celebrate her victory and remember those who did not share the same outcome. I honor the ways my friends pursue their own journeys. I aspire to reward the lean toward health in my own life and the lives of my friends.

Car as Metaphor

The gas tank icon blinked along with the car's beeping, a sure sign of an almost-empty tank. The car almost didn't start. It took three tries, but gas finally got to the engine. I smiled at first and then laughed. That engine and that fuel line are something like certain days I experience. Car as metaphor! Pretty close to running on empty but enough to get me to the pump. The reality of my vehicle matched the assessment from my primary physician, who told me there was nothing wrong with me that good, consistent sleep wouldn't cure. She used the phrase, "running on fumes." And here I was—in my car that reluctantly agreed to start, based upon barely available fumes. Then I just smiled thinking about the long road my life had taken on the way to "the pump."

***

I pulled out of the driveway considering the complexity and paradoxes of my life as an author and artist. What a contradiction it is to have people turning to me, asking, "How?" Like I really know the answers to so many different questions that all begin with "How?" "How do you walk through the tough times while keeping an inspired view?" "How do you manage to keep a writing discipline on a daily basis?" How. Until it begins to sound like howls.

And my primal response to that howling is, "You gotta learn from the rest of the pack and then find your own howl. You can listen to all the other sounds, but ultimately, the sound that rises up from the bottom of your belly and rises up through your upraised throat and spills over your lips is *your* sound—your howl. I can only tell you how I make my noise. It can inspire you to make your own noise. But be assured, it must be your own."

***

I stopped at the light across from the gas station: "the pump." I thought about Brother Lawrence, a fifteenth-century monk who respected liturgy but didn't have much use for it. He called washing dishes his prayer. Serving breakfast to his brother in the best way possible was his prayer. Facing grunt work with grace—prayer. Noticing how my thoughts travel during such times, I wonder if the act of servicing my car would be considered prayer by Brother Lawrence. I suspect the answer is yes.

I begin to fill the tank. Gas is more expensive where I live, and I might be near a more economical option in a day or two. Maybe I should just put in a quarter of a tank. I contemplate thoughts of the hard start less than a mile back. In real time, I recall the advice of my doctor. I decide to fill my tank and let it lead as the metaphor for the day—to demonstrate that while I certainly cannot meet all the obligations in the day, at least I have enough in the moment. My basics are utterly fulfilled and, on some days, that is a celebration.

So Many Systems, Only One You

One only needs to visit a bookstore or the library's Cookbooks/Diet section to see that there are many systems advocating wellness—including many with apparently contradictory recommendations. Learning is good. Considering various methods and protocols is advisable. It is a personal path one walks on the way to one's own optimum level of health. The modern world gives so many opportunities for support and guidance. Even the best intentioned friends are willing to assert that you should do what they have done, since they experienced positive results. But what works for my closest and dearest friends may not work for me. Wellness is a path we walk for ourselves. A map, metaphorically speaking, is helpful. And yet, really, we are ultimately responsible for finding our own best road.

Choose Love

When my dad was first reviewing road safety with me, his fifteen-year-old daughter bearing a driver's permit, he narrated a specific circumstance with a phrase I've often repeated in my mind.

A car jumped its turn at a four-way stop…

"You could have gone—it was your turn—but then that car would have barreled into you. You would have been right, sis, but *dead* right."

He also observed in similar circumstances, "You can choose to be right or alive."

***

Along the way, this driving instruction has been co-opted into a greater spiritual teaching aptly applied to our cooperative journey on the roads of daily experience: "You can be right, or you can be happy." When I recognize my many choices, I often encourage myself with two words: "Choose love." When criticism would get a laugh but hurt some feelings, when a warned-of event comes to pass and "I told you so" is accurate, when directions are asked to be repeated (because they were not listened to the first time)—in so many opportunities for chatter and chastisement, choose love. What builds up positive, loving choice? The conscious effort of choosing love over more judgmental options—rather than offering annoyed correction—allows love to become the basis for sound assessment. Love is an excellent measure in all choices. Wellness is based in many such sound loving measures: moderation, caution, information, balance.

Turn Yourself Toward a Regular Sabbath

Sabbath: it is defined as a period of rest, a set-aside time unique in that it is both separate from what is usual and dedicated to something that is not usual, most often identified as rest, study, or prayer. It is usually one day of turning from one thing and toward something else. The extended sabbatical implies a leave from ordinary experiences for a defined period of time. To sabbatize is to observe a single day of set-aside "Sabbath moments." Taking a sabbatical can be a condensed discipline in perspective, an exercise of turning from that which is less advantageous and turning, perhaps with a prayerful understanding, to a better way of being.

Beyond Desiring, Move to Admiring

*"The secret of happiness is to
admire without desiring."*

—Francis H. Bradley

There are those who would ask me not to address the reality of death
as part of a consideration of health. I think it's where it belongs. Just
as autumn spends its whole season leaning into winter, humans are
born on a trajectory that ends in death. We make an assumption that
each human life's trajectory gets to be long and fair. Both assumptions
are thwarted by many life experiences. Living with intention and
embracing all manner of healthy practices does not shield any one
from the potential of harm or death. They are good practices; best
practices, it could be argued. And still. Death is the companion to our
journey through life.

***

Letter writing has been a lifelong practice. I believe a letter is
a compelling device to express many things that face-to-face
communication doesn't easily accommodate. I recently wrote a
clarifying letter to Death. Of course, I had nowhere to mail it, but the
writing of it did what I intended for myself. It brought me a certain
comfort and clarity.

> Dear Death,
>
> When someone is wrapped in your full embrace, I am
> reminded of the fragility of life. When that someone is
> young, or in the middle of what we anticipate will be a
> long life, we are stunned. The grief is vicious, even. You are
> expected to show up at the end of a journey of many roads

and satisfying miles. In the shock of a quick second, when the circle of companions has a gap, the empty space brings us to our knees. Remembering you can come to any party uninvited is a stark and edgy awareness. May it help me to remember to be kinder, love more readily, and wake to a sense of giftedness for another opportunity to live with intention. Death, perhaps you'll take a little holiday from the planet today? We need a break.

Loving being alive,
—Me.

In function, we are Immortals every moment of our lives—until the second that we are not. It turns out, timing is everything.

Chapter 5

Playfulness
Play with Abandon

"Unleash your silly side from time to time. It enlivens you and offers others unexpected laughs."

—Marci Moore

M arci Moore's words echo one of my life goals. Picture my recent expression of Play as a sixty-three-year-old woman: Pink hair, dancing in my tutu in the parade, being a penguin for Halloween, and wearing crazy leggings to work. Gives you an unexpected laugh, huh? It is what brings me Joy and what re-energizes my batteries to carry on the serious side of life. As a nurse, I know that life can change in an instant. Play is how I live my life without regret.

—Bev Jones

The Key to Brilliance Is Serious: PLAY!

Experts from diverse fields of research are weighing in on the broad benefits of play. When corporate problem solvers engage that playful part of their brains, they discover different roads to solutions. Play invites a different kind of thinking. What many years ago appeared edgy and avant-garde in corporate environments is beginning to be accepted as mainstream protocol. The playroom is no longer limited to primary schools and day-care centers. Play nurtures the body and spirit and gives a fresh wind to the occasionally closed mind.

***

Your life is a piece of music. It could be titled "Transition and Change." Some transitions are marked by events, celebrations, gifts, or symbolism. Others slip into our lives more quietly, mezzo piano—falling gently, leaves of the oak as they change color and flutter to the ground.

***

Today, everything is possible until it isn't; today, I have all I need; today is a celebration of any and all sorts—simply that I am alive. On a day with the absence of so many of my dear ones, being alive is a fierce responsibility. It's not so much that I must live for them, live the life they cannot, but more that with the privilege of breath at waking, of putting my feet to the floor, comes a heightened sense of promise. What will I do with everything that is possible in this day? Embrace the contradiction. The highways of life are not linear. The wide-open lanes of our days travel every which way, in all directions. Just get on the road and play.

Some Day Are Simply Meant for Playing

Take something that another says personally—or laugh. Make "something" of it or make light of it. Today I erred on the side of silliness, and I have many wonderful memories to prove it. This was a day I let my highly sensitive self have most of the day off. It was a day when I was willing to make light of almost everything. This drew out my inner comic and was that ever a lot of fun. I had my friend who was driving us to the store laughing so hard she almost had to pull over to the side of the road for safety. Silliness: some days are simply meant for playing.

***

This phrase was a key element to what is now my "classic" body of work. I started my company with handmade greeting cards. That was my vision: cards that could be posted. I love mail. I love writing to friends and sending things with a real stamp. Receiving mail makes any day almost a holiday. My commitment to meaningful greeting cards came naturally to me, just as naturally as the longing for the water on a particular cerulean-blue-sky-just-out-of-the-watercolor-tube day in July on the coast of Oregon. In the early years of my company, I was the all and everything. I staffed the retail/showroom space while I did all the production work for the wholesale element. It was a Saturday, and the earnestness of my posted retail hours and the obligation to fulfill the orders awaiting my hands were singing loudly. There was a louder message. It was the symphony of summer. My wetsuit was in my closet at work. My boogie board was in my vehicle. I grabbed a discarded card prototype and wrote, by way of explanation for the closed door, "Some days are simply meant for playing." I taped it to the door and gleefully spent the remainder of my day playing in the sea. I returned to work the following day, refreshed and ready to create! I was surprised to find five "orders" scooted under the door in response to the "poster" that was taped up as a message to my visitors. A day of play produced the product that would come to be the hallmark of my product offering and the basis for a lifetime of satisfying work.

Celebration Has Many Outfits but Always Wears the Same Comfortable Shoes

Hospitality and holiday need not be governed by a calendar. There are many occasions over the course of life that call for celebration. I am most happy when I am creating an event for no particular reason at all on a rather ordinary Thursday. Being grateful to be alive or having a memory that works or an arm that can spin in giant circles is enough of a reason to celebrate.

Sit, Stay, Heal: How One Big Black Dog Trained my Heart

I was flying home after visiting my dear friends: the family that had adopted my sweet Labrador retriever named Judah. A set of earlier life circumstances had led to placing Judah in a home where he would have children to herd and a much greater opportunity for exercise and doing all the things that big dogs love to do. He was absolutely thrilled with his new family. And they loved having Judah as part of their pack.

My heart was very heavy as the plane began winging back to my own home. My visit had been to say good-bye to the dog that had taught me so much and had done such good work for two families. Judah was dying of lung cancer. I thought my grief would cry itself a river…right there on the plane. My seat mate asked if I was all right, and all I could muster was, "My dog is dying." She understood immediately, patting my hand with the quiet compassion that understanding brings.

***

I started thinking about all the gifts of joy and play this amazing dog had brought into my life. And I decided to answer the void of my loss with a list of all the lessons that dog had delivered to my heart. Even in my sorrow, Judah led me to focus on the good right in front of me, just as he naturally always did. So here's some of the list, as I made it on that flight home. Though Judah did indeed leave the planet just days later, his lessons live on, and I will share a few of them with you. They are playfully titled, "Sit, Stay, Heal," because that is how Judah trained me and healed me over the years. Play wasn't at the very top of Judah's priority list, but it was very close.

***

Be clear on your priorities:

1. Food

2. Treats

3. See previous

4. Rolling in the grass

5. Playing with your pack and yummies (see first and second)

Be fully engaged with the task in front of you.
When you're tired of running, just sit down.
When you're tired of turning in circles chasing your tail, stop.

When you have an itch, go to the best scratcher.

You really have to like someone to share your food with them.
The enthusiasm behind the tail is more important than the things the
tail knocks over.

Engage in pleasures ravenously.
Even seemingly undesirable activities can be turned into adventure.
The risk of playing too hard and getting hurt is worth it if you're
playing with a really cool dog. Play until you can't. Play, romp, bite,
roll, sniff, sit on each other, wrestle, run, rest. Repeat.
The present moment is where all the good stuff happens. Play grows
in the soil of a cheerful heart.

Chapter 6

Gratitude
Laugh

"Happiness lives in a grateful heart."

—Jean Martell

L iving with gratitude opens my heart to happiness. It allows me to see the world from a positive perspective. Laughter and gratitude together are the best! Laughter came easily to my good friend and I throughout our forty-year friendship. We'd laugh until we cried at the littlest of things. When she was diagnosed with cancer, laughter became very good medicine! We also had many heartfelt conversations during her illness. Before she passed away, she shared that she'd like to return as a hawk because they are beautiful, strong, and free. As I sat with her during one of her last days, I looked out the window to see a beautiful hawk circling nearby. I pictured her spirit soaring right along with it. In the years since her passing, often when I'm struggling and missing her, a hawk will fly overhead or show up in an unexpected place. I feel her presence. The gratitude I feel for those encounters adds happiness to my life. Feeling grateful for the miracle of life each day is a choice I make. I firmly believe this to be true:

"A miracle is not defined by an event.
A miracle is defined by gratitude."

—Kate Baestrup

Recognize the miracles, laugh, have gratitude, and be happy.

—Jean Martell

Talk About Everything That's Gone Right in the Day

I hold gratitude deeply. It rumbles around in my soul, and it comes tumbling out as laughter. The capacity to experience gratitude in all circumstances is tied experientially to laughter and laughing. In moments when I am disconnected from my sense of gratitude, laughter is a path to walk me there. Laughter opens the window of perspective that then allows gratitude to blow into the musty corners of my being. Perhaps laughter is tied to a different quality in your life experience? What qualities does laughter draw out in you?

***

My good friend Steve Maraboli said to me, "It's the best kind of tired when, at the end of the day, you've left it all on the field and all your pockets are empty." This is not a negative statement, but a reference to giving your all. Steve advocates a life where you put your shoulder into the vision you want to craft for yourself and push. The empty pockets he is referencing are about compromise. He knows that the way you avoid regret is to pour as much of yourself out into the things that matter. The number of things the world wants you to pay attention to is large. So I'll highlight a point: it is being engaged in the things that matter most to you in a single day, not the litany of priorities of others or all of the things the media might highlight. The way news is delivered is fodder for a very difficult conversation. "The news" carries such an intrinsic negative message that when we have news of the positive sort, we must qualify it by saying, "Now here's the good news."

Cultivate the habit of telling friends what has gone right, what is worth noting for its joy and verve and lesson. Join in conversations with, "Something like that happened to me once," and if it must be about a disaster, then make sure the story you tell includes something about a disaster averted, not just a disaster. Bad news is, of course, present in every life experience. It knows how to take up plenty of room on its own. I figure, why make even larger space for it by telling tales of woes? I'd rather aspire to speaking of all that has gone well.

***

Even in facing the most difficult circumstances with my friend Donna when she was engaged with two different types of invasive cancer, we found the road of laughter connected us to gratitude. She is the first to acknowledge that her sense of humor and finding things to laugh about paved her pathway of healing and recovery. I remember vividly our jolly exchange the day her doctor suggested nuclear medicine (literally injecting her with radioactive isotopes) as a treatment for her stage three cancer. Pondering the implications, she seriously asked her doctor, "Does this mean I won't have to use my night light for a few weeks?" Laughter has allowed Donna to see things that have gone well, even on some of the worst days of her illness.

***

My friend Mollyshannon recounted to me what elements of a public presentation of mine had really stayed with her. As an accomplished presenter, she could have offered me a critique of my work. She could have numbered the times I used "um" in a sentence or paused to find my place in my notes. What she did was identify all the things I did right. I appreciated hearing how she heard my words as she quoted back to me.

***

You tell the tale of your life by the stories you repeat in your days. Does this mean my life is absent of difficulties? Of course not. I have health challenges and issues with finances and friends who are ill. My life is filled with elements that are less than ideal. But that is not the story I tell. That is not what I spend my emotional investments on. The story I tell is the story of recovery, discovery, and uncovering. Those are the stories I repeat in my days. The really good stories bear repeating and those are the stories of laughter and lessons that lead me to my sense of gratitude.

Change Your Story

Consider writing on the theme, "You Wouldn't Believe What Happened Next…" and fill in the rest of the story with laughter. It's very interesting that the easiest tale to carry is one about something that went wrong. Joy is everywhere. It takes open eyes to see it and an open heart to appreciate it.

***

I promised myself to see and write words. I was due to complete a project, and I was pretty sure at the start of the day that I was promising to fold myself utterly into my task of composing. Ahhhh. I also told myself that meant no second-guessing nor turning away of ideas, and that everything would be considered. And all of those ideas that wanted to be considered came knocking—quickly. They arrived as if by a magic invitation. Dang. It's just that I thought I'd invited words that would be written in my book, and what I got instead were words of adventure and joy lived out in the experience of my day. Rather than turning to expectation and disappointment, that nasty one-two punch, I opened myself to the whole winter solstice day. I was gifted with words—better ones than what I could have imagined at the start of my creative day. I had the heart to see the words that came courting. They indeed were everywhere, just not dressed as I initially anticipated. They were dressed in experience and fun opportunity. And so it is with laughter. We all experience things that are only funny when we look back on them. Joy occurs when we can laugh in the midst of the experience as it unfolds.

***

In her unfolding recovery, my friend Donna hopped on an electric-scooter shopping cart. She'd been bedbound for over two weeks, and her cabin fever got the best of her and her caregiver. They went for what seemed like a simple shopping expedition. Donna quipped that she was already nuclear-powered by virtue of the medicine that had been pumped into her veins, and she charged off on that scooter with the same high-powered verve! Even though the end-cap display of canned green beans was the visible evidence of the tight corner she turned, and product was scattered all over the grocery store floor, she could not keep from laughing. Her caregiver slipped aisles away in an effort to control her laughing fit. Even the store employee whose job it would be to recover all the cans saw the humor. It has produced a new nickname, and we're talking about the source of an excellent children's story found in her expanded tales of "Scooter G. Beanes."

Relax into the Natural Embrace of the Day

Resentment can boil up out of too many restraints. There are certain tasks that modern life requires of us. Fulfilling those tasks is part of what people call adulting. To live an obligation-free life means you understand the need to serve the debts of history and the promise of the future; bring harm to no one; live with profound meaning and positive impact; be willing to see an old thing in a new way; and be willing to be financially rewarded for sincere and authentic effort. Stand ready to be utterly healthy and completely responsible to wellness; cultivate and maintain a strong immune system and a consistent energy; embrace the structures that guarantee strength and wellness and continually build upon them with information and knowledge. Express gratitude for all the influences in life. Ease into the natural embrace and flow of the day and maintain a cadence that is realistic and reflects your fundamental intentions.

***

A revived threat arrived in the mail, announcing intended legal action on an issue I thought was long ago resolved and put to rest. There are issues impacting my health and wellness that remain unresolved. And yet I had a great day. I took appropriate action on those larger issues and then gave myself to the next thing in my day. I have lived another way—the way in which the yet unresolved issues cloud my joy and muddy the colors of my art. I choose this other way, the way that does not gamble with what may be but rather invests in what is. I relaxed into the natural embrace of the day. I enjoyed the many gifts that came my way. I recognize that those challenges will again call my name. And when they do, I will answer them at that time, in that day. In this way, framed in gratitude, I am able to put even unpleasant things, hard things, in context. In this way, all things get their place, their time, and their due.

"Pour a warm cup of gratitude, sweetened with laughter, and prepare for another day."

—Mary Anne Radmacher

Chapter 7

Perspective
Fail with Enthusiasm

*"Failure is a mindset, not a circumstance. I let
my experiences strengthen me. You think I fell on
my face, but I'm down here doing pushups."*

—Steve Maraboli

W e often have a diluted sense of self; we do not see the magnitude of the greatness inside of us. As a result, most people live within the parameters of the lowest part of their life; they dwell in the basement of their capability.

When you have a small picture of yourself, it distorts the size of the problems and challenges you face. You become easily intimidated and even more easily deterred from following your desired success. You look at mistakes as final and failures as unworthiness. You see a small you and a BIG everything else. The vision of yourself is distorted and the efficiency of your journey is burdened.

You are a reflection of greatness; don't lose sight of that! There have been countless challenges that you thought were bigger than you, but you're still here. They have not defeated you, they have not stopped you, and even if you didn't realize it, they had to bow to your innate superiority.

Keep your dream alive. Keep your relationship alive. Keep your career alive. Keep your goal alive. Live big! You have not been rejected; you have been redirected. Delayed, but not denied. You are greater than you can ever imagine! Let your journey be fueled and your body be nourished by your victorious past and move forward in the direction of your magnificent dreams. You are worthy; live accordingly.

—Steve Maraboli

Willingness to Succeed Partners with the Willingness to Fail

My dad used to tell me laughingly that on some mornings just climbing out of bed can be an act of success, even courage. Am I without failure? Am I fearless? No, hardly. I wrestle with the uninvited visitor of fear. Unanswered, inexplicable medical issues raised fear within me. I went through a period of time in which I became increasingly ill. The cause was elusive, and no remedy seemed available. I stepped out of the grip of fear and started exploring, guessing, risking new things, quitting old patterns. It worked. The risks paid off immediately, and my health continues to improve. In large part, the whole of my life has been a risk. Absent safety in my home life (during my childhood and occasionally as an adult), my ventures outside were all risks: starting a business, expansion, shrinking, expansion without a safety net, and starting again. It was worth it—all of it. I hold no regret. How could I regret any of it? I love where I stand today, and it stands to reason that I cannot regret all the ways of risk that brought me to this very place.

***

Every possibility, each opportunity can stand at the threshold with the companion question, "What if?" Allowing for risk has been the best response to that question time and again. Confidence and curiosity are inner coaches whispering in my ear, saying, "You'll never know unless you try." Being closely acquainted with the intentions of your life makes risk more palatable. When you assess the possibility before you and see the ways it aligns with your intention, it is easier to take the first step—and the steps that come after.

***

Psssst. Go ahead, make a promise to yourself. Risk it.

*"Those who dare to fail miserably
can achieve greatly."*

—John F. Kennedy

***

A pendulum swings. It's a law of physics: equal and opposite reactions. Perhaps said more truthfully from my experience, each great success may be partnered with an equally great failure. It's often true, but not always. Perhaps the real partner in the equation is the willingness to fail on the way to great achievement. The willingness to walk that road reveals another way—it shines a light on another path. That willingness, often called risk, accompanies the finest outreach. That outreach is rewarded by applying your own intentions daily.

Close That Ledger

Many people are happy to recount, with specificity, the number of times that they have succeeded. It's more difficult to find a leader who is willing to celebrate and teach from the numbers of times that they have failed. It's tempting for the inner critic that travels with so many of us to provide a detailed accounting of such times: tried and failed; tried and failed. Of that voice, I often request, "Learn first. Close the ledger."

***

Balance occurs in the whole, not within the parts. Searching for balance in the specifics of the little bits yields small return. At low tide, with long mud flats, it is hard to imagine a river lapping the edges of the banks. Yet in a moon cycle, there is evidence of the balance—the ebb and flow—of the tide waters.

***

There is imbalance in a moment. That moment of seeming asymmetry, taken as an important part of the greater view, becomes a part of an account of balance. Know that you can close the ledger book! Look up and be present to the experience in front of you. When you have time for a backward glance, you will be surprised at the equilibrium, the symmetry, the balance, written into the lines of the ledger of your heart when you were not looking. Parity occurs in the big picture, not the small snapshots.

Broken

Waiting to heal. Swimming in a sea that feels like failure and so close to danger that most people cannot even see. Uncomfortably close to the rocks just below the surface. Broken. Wondering what's wrong. Uncertain if the fault lies within or in the stars, or if there even is any fault to be found. I see you, and I understand because I have been broken. I know there is a way to see the lesson in the lie, a way to see the future possible in the middle of what feels like fantastic failure. Come here. Swim here. We'll go together and push through the waves. We will make for the shore. The view from there holds no blame, only hope.

Heart Shaped Rocks

There they sit on a shelf, the tall heart poised, prepared, solid. Sturdy for the leaning of the one I've wrapped with strands of gold and shades of the color of the sea. These hearts remind me of the miles one must walk to discover the treasures that the sea willingly offers up. The treasures come without prejudice and are available to the first person who demonstrates the ability to be present and to notice.

When I look up from my work, when I am inclined to rest, to stretch, I see them. I see them afresh, and the iconic impact delivers messages of love, beauty, and commitment. These hearts of stone do not call me to be hard but to be willing—to let the sea of life pour over me, again and again, and create a canyon of depth and insight. They do not promise that I will never suffer hurt or injury but rather assure me that I will thrive because of my choice to show up, willing to give and ready to receive a gift.

When Angels Cry (A Myth That Might Be True)

"You know a lot about the world, don't you, Grandpa?" Jen's grandfather nodded. It didn't matter how many times they made their way through the sea grass, down the shifting sand path to the shore, he always managed to point out something new.

"Aw, Jen, when you've been around as long as me, you pick up some knowledge along the way."

He'd told her lots of stories, even the story of why her dad had given her two names, both starting with J. Grandpa said her dad had learned fairly young the importance of being able to turn around on a path—just like the curves in the Js of her names, Jennifer Jane. Neither her dad nor her grandpa had ever told her *why* it was so important that her dad had learned to turn around…just that he had. They wouldn't be turning around any time soon this morning. This was a good path, and they walked it together almost every Monday morning. Just before the path leveled out, she saw one of her most sought-after finds. "Already!" Grandpa observed.

"It's going to be a good day." Jen agreed as she slipped the heart-shaped rock into her pocket. "Will you, Grandpa? Will you tell it again?"

He knew that she was asking for the story of how heart rocks came to be. If he timed it just right, the telling would last their whole walk. "Well, little sister…"

Jennifer loved the way he began this story. He began all his stories the very same way. He told her that in the face of any Great Story, we all become a brother and a sister because we are all equal when standing before any Great Truth.

***

"Long ago, in the World That Was, the Elders depended on the angels to tend everything. In those days, angels were not like the ones we think of today. They were more like a force of farmers tending the whole earth. Each was responsible for specific areas of caretaking."

Jennifer knew the kinds of questions to ask at just the right moments. Her grandfather insisted that knowing the kinds of questions to ask was just as important as choosing the best story to tell. "Do you mean that each angel had a small field like our strawberry patch?"

"Not quite. It was much bigger than that. It's truer to say they each tended many fields, and that what they planted was unlike anything we plant. They were fields of Dreams. These angels were responsible for planting and growing Ideas. Notions. Highly Unlikely Possibilities. Amazing Potentials. They planted and tended the essence, the core of a thing. They cultivated and tended for Great Discoveries. They planted trusting that someday, when the right time and the right person or persons came together, a particular crop would be harvested. And that's just how it worked. Fields came to fruition for the likes of Madam Curie, Mary Cassatt, Copernicus, and all the women and men who helped them discover the work that was planted in a field of dreams, long ago."

***

There's only one thing about Grandfather's story that ever changed. It was one of the reasons why Jennifer asked him to tell it so many times. Grandpa switched who he named as harvesters. She'd repeat their names to help her remember. After they got home, she would look up each name in her family's Big Books to see what Great Idea they had harvested from the fields of Dreams. Some people he mentioned had harvested more than one Great Idea.

***

The story paused because Grandfather paused in front of the largest rock on this beach. It was called Heart Break Rock. People came from all over the world to photograph it. It was actually shaped like a giant heart and was surrounded by a scattering of smaller rocks that looked like they had broken off and tumbled down. Jennifer had learned years earlier that the rocks were called monoliths. Many people thought that's how the monolith had gotten its name—for the rocks that broke off the big heart. But Jen knew better—the history of the name was found in Grandpa's story. The wind was picking up, so Grandpa turned them around to head back home. He continued the story.

"A great dissatisfaction began to rise among the angels. They'd been planting and tending for as long as any of them could remember: Always planting; always tending; and then always watching others do the harvesting. One of them rose up and spoke out, saying what many of them had been thinking and feeling but hadn't had the nerve to say. He said, 'What's the use? What are we doing? We toil. We are diligent. We plant. We plant some more. And then we tend and wait. We work hard on these ideas, these visions, these dreams, and what do we get out of it? Someone else gets to harvest our work. We get no credit and never enjoy the satisfaction of making a harvest ourselves.'

"Such words of discontentment had never been voiced among the angels before. It shook them all deeply. Even the angels who experienced the most unfettered joy in watching the Great

Discoverers come upon a dream field started experiencing the rumbling sadness of this frustration. The melancholy came upon them all first as a reverberation, next like a growing echo, and then it exceeded the ease of their hearing with the clap of a harsh *boom*."

Jennifer couldn't resist. "That's what we now call *thunder*!"

"That's right, Jennifer. That's a different story for another walk!" They laughed, happily holding the thought of another story and another walk.

"The resounding sorrow rolled over the angels until they all came to an unbearable sense of sadness. It was the sorrow that they would never be the ones to realize any of the dreams they worked so hard to sow. Their heartbreak spread, and soon, all over the world, angels were weeping. As their tears struck the soil of the earth, each teardrop turned to stone. Each stone was different according to the angel whose tears fell, and yet they were each shaped like a heart.

"The Eldest Elder called all of the angels together. She called them from all corners of the world to a gathering, right here—right here on this long expanse of shore. From all parts, they came. As the leader raised her voice, the angels became still. 'I hear your sorrow. I feel your sorrow as it rumbles, shaking the sky. I understand the ache you experience at planting dreams you will never reap, tending this sweet fruit of ideas that you will never taste yourself.

" 'You must be careful lest this magnificent melancholy make you as hard as the tears you weep. On your behalf, only and ever this once, I will grieve this Great Grief for you and I will answer your sadness and breaking hearts in a way you can always see and remember.'

"She rose up, high above them all. She allowed herself to feel the hurt of planting and sowing, tending and working, and never personally holding the reward. She considered and held all the Dreams waiting to be discovered that would be doubted, undreamt, or walked over. She considered all the Waiting Ideas that would be dismissed with doubts such as, "What's the use?" and their realization doomed because a failure looked like an ending, not another beginning. She wept with Great Sorrow. Her grief poured one teardrop from her eye, and, as it struck the earth, it became the monolith we now know as Heart Break Rock. And from the force of its landing, smaller shards of sorrow broke off and surrounded the large rock. Each magnificent teardrop formed monoliths that stand to this day, all around the world.

"The enormity of her tears recalled all the angels back to their Great Work. Even the one among them who had voiced the discontent was inspired by the beauty of the giant rocks. As they began to call to mind the nobility of their purpose, the Eldest Elder finished, saying, 'This great stone is set to remind you of your calling, your true purpose. When the thunder of sorrow comes rumbling, you need not weep for long. You can hear it and know there is an opportunity to return to your fields. There is always a chance to—' "

"Turn AROUND!" Jennifer finished, jumping up and down, "Just like the curve in the Js of my names."

"So, what happens next?" Grandpa asked Jennifer.

"You tell it. You tell, Grandpa!" So he did.

"The Eldest Elder turned to the angel who had first given voice to his frustration and doubt. She walked to him with the love that comes from understanding. She offered him no scolding or shame, she simply stood close to him and asked what had been learned. That angel said, 'I know better now that it does not fall to me to realize results. It is my joy and reward to plant the seed knowing that someone else will pick the fruit of that idea or dream.' It was clear to those looking that this angel was inspired by the seed of a new notion, and they watched as he rushed to sow his newest idea in many fields. That which the angel sowed that day has been gleaned by Dreamers from around the world over many centuries.

"Robert Louis Stevenson came upon one of the fields that was planted that day. He explained what he found this way, 'Don't judge each day by the harvest you reap, but by the seeds that you plant.' A second-generation farmer named Nelson Henderson in a place called Minnesota wrote, 'The true meaning of life is to plant trees under whose shade you do not expect to sit.' Wisdom so old no one can remember who first said it suggests that the best time to plant a tree was twenty years ago, and the next best time is now. Sacred and honorable texts use the idea of planting as a way to inspire giving to the generations to come without thought of any immediate or personal benefit."

The wind whooshed just as Grandfather ended the story, and then they were almost to the path leading back to Grandfather's home. As if it were the perfect punctuation to the story, Jennifer pushed her toes into the sand to brace against the gusts and she felt a stone. When she wiped away the thin layer of sand, there was her second heart-shaped rock. "Oh, Grandpa! It's a gift for remembering what happens when angels cry."

"That's the best part of the story, Jennifer. That is what happened long ago, that one time when the angels cried with such heartbreak. Their teardrops turned to heart-shaped stones back then. Now, it's different. Those heart stones used to be easy to find, too numerous to count. The reason they aren't so easily discovered now is there are fewer of them. Those stones are witness that there is always hope to find another way." Jennifer's mouth was wide open in disbelief. She thought she knew the story almost word for word, and now she found there was something she had never heard before. She looked up at her grandfather in surprise and breathlessly asked, "What? Just once? So then why would an angel cry *now*, and what happens when they do?"

Grandpa looked down at Jen and tucked her wind-wild hair behind her ears.

"My sweet girl, angels cry now because they understand and feel deeply when they see hurts and loss in the world. They weep at the divide that peoples of the earth experience because they choose to see their differences rather than the ways they are common to each other. In these times, when angels cry, their tears fall on hearts that are broken and mend them in that broken place."

This made Jennifer feel very safe, knowing that if her heart ever broke, there was a way for it to mend. Jennifer nodded quietly as they started up the path toward home. She imagined taking her initials, the two Js, and turning them on end, flipping one over backward and joining them at the top and bottom. She loved imagining her two Js turned into a heart.

She slipped her hand into her grandpa's hand and they walked home quietly, each busy thinking their own thoughts.

Because

Because I call it a lesson rather than a failure,

Because I call it a challenge rather than a crisis,

Because I look at hardship as opportunity rather than obstacle, because at the end of a matter, I ask, "What will I learn from this to make me better?"

Because I take a deep breath and do the difficult thing first, because my courage does not depend on the weather, the economic forecast, or the winds of whim, because I know the significant elements in my day are laughter, learning, and applying my finest efforts to each endeavor, because of all these things, each morning holds promise and every day passed is a success.

Chapter 8

Forgiveness
Choose with No Regret

*"By opening our hearts and forgiving others,
we clear the path to forgiving ourselves."*

—Caren Albers

I spent nearly sixty years clinging to stories about my wrongs and the wrongs done to me. I had no problem advising others to "Let it go." "L-I-G" I wrote and said with full confidence and authority. Finally, in my own healing, I took my own advice. I realized that if I couldn't open my heart and forgive others, I would never get to celebrate the gift of my own forgiveness. So I made the choice to scale that mountain, and on the other side I found the peace, ease, and clarity I had been seeking all this time.

—Caren Albers

Hardly Ever

"Staying in the moment means you hardly ever have to forgive yourself—or anyone else—or ask for forgiveness."

—Jan Johnson

Key in Johnson's phrase are the words "hardly ever." This is not a rigid formulation. The lines between choosing with no regret and offering forgiveness to yourself—or others—can be fuzzy. I offer up that they are in partnership. Your choices stand, etched in history. Regrets aside, there is no change to be made. Forgiveness allows you to embrace your choices and accept them in the context of where you stand today.

A Gift of Grace to Myself

"Forgive all who have offended you, not for them, but for yourself."

—Harriet Nelson

My friend Caren Albers shares her experience with this very grace. She shares with you…

When I was a child, I would laugh and say about a friend, "We're in a fight, but she doesn't know it." I thought it was clever and funny never thinking that withholding forgiveness could have a negative impact. Forgiveness and I share a long history. I spent decades trying to forgive my parents for a childhood that left me feeling scarred and wanting. I longed for healing and happiness, but my failed attempts at forgiveness left me feeling worse than when I started, and I didn't know why. A fortunate stroke of serendipity happened while studying the latest brain science on recall and memory. As I searched for ways to improve my aging brain and failing memory, I gained new insights into how the brain works and an understanding of the impact of forgiveness.

What I found was that during recall, the brain "replays" a pattern of neural activity that was originally generated in response to a particular event, echoing the brain's perception of the real event. In fact, there is no real solid distinction between the act of remembering and the act of thinking. When we remember something, we relive the event with all the accompanying emotions of the initial event. All the "somebody did somebody wrong" things, "not my fault" things, and everything we haven't found a way to forgive ourselves or others for can cause us pain by simply recalling them.

A few years back, my heart ached from a falling-out with a soul friend. Our attempts to heal the hurt failed, and eventually she asked me not to contact her. Wounded and heartbroken, I complied. Every time I remembered the incident, I would be right back there in the center of all my emotions. Even looking at gifts she gave me brought pain, so I started packing things up to donate. One was a purple jacket.

After a time, we found our way back to each other and forgiveness. On a day when a cold snap hit, I went looking for a jacket. On the closet floor, I found the bag I'd intended to donate, and inside was the purple jacket. Trying it on flooded me with warmth and all the good emotions from the positive neural pathways created by our reconciliation. That now defines us.

Imagine how different our lives would be if we forgave everyone.

This science empowered me. It taught me that you can only hurt me once. After that, I'm responsible if I withhold forgiveness and continue hurting myself with a memory.

Forgiveness is an act of self-love. Do it for *you*!

—Caren Albers

Celebrate Seeing the Door to Change

To march through life announcing we want control, don't take well to change, and don't like surprises is a formula for continual conflict. The soil of struggle is the playground for change. And if you've ever seen a single flower blooming in a crack where it has pushed through the cement—or a wildflower blossoming in the snow, then you know life is full of surprises—all kinds of them: a promotion, loss of a child, a gift delivered unexpectedly, or an unkind word. Surprises are like licorice: they come in many different colors—and flavors.

I celebrate seeing the door to change. Seeing the opportunity helps me be less resistant to it. Viewing myself as a perennial student informs me that I have so much to learn. I used to listen to anyone saying almost anything, nodding my head and asserting, "I know. I know." I was seeking the stamp of approval for already knowing what they were trying to tell me. I have come to recognize the value of not knowing, of listening to words and wondering, even if they are familiar, if I can hear something new in their lyrics. I am breathless, too, at the door of change swinging open and hitting me on the nose. I keep my eyes on that door—so I can happily walk toward it and help it open. Open safely!

The Road to Restorative Sleep

*"In the space of stillness following a
long exhale—our truth speaks."*

—Caren Albers

This offers an understanding of the instruction, "Take a deep breath," which must come before the metabolic grasp of the long exhalation.

That which I hold…releases.
That which I hide…reveals.
That which I inhibit…becomes relevant.

I exhaled into my sleep and breathed out betrayals and sorrows, assumptions and bright, shiny bitterness that I carried around in a spiritual jewelry case. Why? Deceived by their sparkle, I thought they were pretty, worthy of my attention, or precious. In the light cast by an encompassing morning, all these things are seen with a more accurate metaphor—covered with slimy, hanging moss usually reserved for the waterlogged underbelly of an old dock.

In the drying breath of the long exhale, in the truth of my own stillness, I see those insidious hitchhikers of my soul, and I no longer offer them transport. In my exhalation, they are borne away on the wind of my deep breath—my breath, which is strengthened and empowered by my desire to move beyond the willfully carried encumbrances of my past into the ecstatic ease of being present to this forgiving moment.

Forgive, Move On, Learn

There are people who were once close. We grew apart. I moved on. There have been people, chosen intimates whose choices appeared as betrayal and I let myself walk away, freely, forgiving myself and forgiving them. One of the ways I redeem these difficult experiences is to chart and record all I have learned from them. Here's a short list:

- Being crazy doesn't exclude being kind, funny, and possessing elements of grace.

- The right tools invite skill: never apologize for someone else's mistake.

- There is always a way to be kind; find it. Anything can be a reason for a party.

- What you declared as a lie in me was actually me learning to speak my truth.

- Unconditional love looks as simple as a long walk to a dog.

- Your no becomes my yes.

- We are responsible to each other, not for each other.

- Just because you can't see the world from under that blanket does not mean the world is invisible.

- Lonely sometimes masquerades as mean.

- Forgiveness often precedes gratitude.

Does Forgiveness Imply Tolerating Bad Behavior?

I began the shift years ago, before I was even aware of the specter of martyrdom. I finally understood that my older brother wasn't behaving like everyone else's older brother. I finally grasped that he was harming me. And I hit him with a right hook that sprained my wrist. I can't remember the precise harm I brought to his bloody nose, but I know I hurt him. There's no fun in purposely bringing harm and there is a right time to defend yourself. I no longer feared him, and I was prepared to defend myself again, and that was clear to him. After that, he stopped hurting me.

In my twenties, another shift occurred. I read about ACoA: Adult Children of Alcoholics. I thought I was so unique in my challenges and pain, and then I looked around and understood there were millions of "us": souls raised in the shadow of alcoholism but without the alcohol in our own veins to dull the pain. So unhealthy structures to dull, protect, and hide became the medication, instead of drugs or alcohol. These behavioral addictions are challenging to kick because on the outside they make me look like: A) the nice one; B) the good girl; C) the giver; D) the negotiator.

In truer terms, they should be called: A) doormat; B) martyr; C) dupe—pouring an endless pitcher; D) compromiser. Certainly, these are less endearing titles but sometimes more accurate. I continue to understand and name these behaviors as they rise up from my history.

***

Well. Books have been written on this subject and the subjects that evolve out of it. As for me, I won't be writing a book on it anytime soon. I find it as elusive as a beautiful butterfly: almost winging to a landing on my outstretched hand…and then, floating away on the wind. Sometimes I get it. Sometimes I don't. I continue to practice the boundary setting that enables me to see and say, "This is not okay." But what I do know is this… I've had the separate bedroom and the divorce that followed. I have been through some of the challenges that Eleanor Roosevelt faced. And Eleanor is right. No one can make me feel poorly about myself without my permission.

How about you? Who's in charge of how you feel about yourself?

Every Ending Draws the Line for the Next Beginning

The trees: the trees do so many important things—without effort, their tree-ness is adequate. They stand tall, provide home to many other life-forms, oxygenate, hold fast the ground, absorb lightning, and allow time and natural elements to heal wounds to their being. As they bend in the wind, there's no tree saying, "I must be more flexible." They are just as flexible as they are—no more, no less. As they bend in the wind, there's no tree saying, "I must be more proactive." They allow endings and beginnings, the natural cycle, and each does what they do best: be a tree. New evidence supports what Tolkein and many others long supposed. Trees communicate and help each other thrive. Like the trees, we do not need to learn these lessons all on our own.

***

"He that cannot forgive others breaks the bridge over which he himself must pass."

—George Herbert

Forgiveness. When the circumstances requiring forgiveness from others involve continual, consistent bad behavior, it creates a conundrum. It is a challenging balance between letting go with forgiveness and finding a way not to engage with unacceptable behavior. Forgiveness is not to be confused with tolerance or accommodation. One friend of mine feared forgiveness. He thought it meant saying, "I forgive you for breaking my nose," and then standing there so his nose could be broken again.

Forgiveness for behaviors doesn't imply continued toleration of the behavior. Forgiveness dissolves the resentment, releases the anger, and resolves potential bitterness. Forgiveness allows the clarity of acceptance of circumstance to seep in, or sometimes rush in. This underscores that forgiveness is always self-serving. It is an invitation to personal freedom from the shackles that tie one to unfavorable conditions or actions. Forgiveness does not require that one remain in untenable circumstances.

Dealing with continual poor practices is one thing. Forgiveness is quite another. Rather than the offended person becoming inured to the offense, forgiveness lets fresh air into the murky, musty room of muddled thinking and breathes renewed lucidity into the challenging circumstance(s). My friend, Patti Digh, created a sticker. She sent me several dozens of them. It read, "I forgive you. Now go far away."

Choosing with no regret and forgiveness are inextricably tied. It does not mean I can declare that all the choices in my life have been good ones. Hardly. I can say that I love where I stand today. In that, I have no regret for the choices I have made. Those choices have all conspired to bring me to this moment. An intersection of loving my present and forgiving my past is a place of balance and peace.

A Blessing

"In the quiet of this day, may forgiveness invite you to rise on the greatness of your spirit, and may your renewed hopes fly on the wings of unfettered possibility."

—Mary Anne Radmacher

Chapter 9

Enthusiasm
Continue to Learn

*"Enthusiasm allows your mind to
be open to possibilities."*

—Arla DeField

E nthusiasm resonates with me viscerally. It is the quality and outlook that embodies how I embrace life for all it is worth. That is how I aspire to live my life. Choosing enthusiasm is not always easy; however, I believe it is always the best. Enthusiasm is not just the spice of life; it is what drives zestful living.

Enthusiasm allows your mind to be open to possibilities not yet seen or known; it allows you to approach each experience as a student, looking to learn and absorb and live life to the fullest. Without an enthusiastic outlook, actions are drudgery, living is a chore, new experiences and situations are scary and overwhelming.

When you embrace living with enthusiasm, your mindset is oriented toward growth and each day is an adventure, bringing new experiences and situations with the opportunity to wring out every last drop of joy!

—Arla DeField

Begin Each Day Aligned with Your Enthusiastic Purpose

Being connected to your enthusiasm is a great deal of fun, brings vibrancy and zest to each part of the day, and throws the doors of your experience wide open. There are some requirements. You must be willing to set aside ego and any attachment you have to looking smart or sophisticated. Your interests must lie in discovery and presence, not appearance and assessment. The instant the familiar question, "What will people think?" is asked, enthusiasm evaporates. Enthusiasm prefers the company of freedom and unselfconsciousness. A service provider and I speak often about her childhood dream of being a dancer. Her dream was deferred in adulthood and traded for more practical pursuits. Regularly, we make the case for dance finding a place in her every day. She returned the compliment recently, observing my "dancing hands" and helping me remember the pleasure of movement with a ribbon tied with a swivel to the end of a stick, a popular children's toy and a device used by dancers around the world.

"Oh, yes!" I recalled all the ways that the ribbons can be moved. It is like writing with color in the air. I made a note to myself: find one. And I did. Wandering through a toy store, I came upon them unexpectedly (seizing serendipity is another favorite thing of enthusiasm). One for each hand came home with me. Parked on the ferry dock, I unwrapped one ribbon while standing alongside my car. When I teach journal writing to children, we do an exercise called "air writing." It's like finger painting, only without the paint and paper—we write in the air. Adding a ribbon turns it into skywriting. And right there on the ferry dock I began waving the ribbons in patterns in the air, oblivious. It took a man walking by, kindly laughing and observing, "You are having entirely too much fun," for me to be aware of the stares and smiles from the people in the dozens of cars around me. Both were returned with a shrug and a smile. With no embarrassment, I resumed my discovery process of all the ways those ribbons would have me move it.

***

If you feel the need for assistance or tutoring in this celebration of your enthusiasm, there are two readily available resources. Hang out with some local three- or four-year-olds, or a big ol' dog in moist, fresh-mown grass. In those classrooms, you will learn 'most everything you need to know to begin celebrating your native enthusiasm.

Learn as If Your Life Depends on It—Because It May

The adults with the best study skills are the most successful because they learn from all their life experiences—they show up and listen even if the particular experience is not an enjoyable instructor. Take notes, ask questions (especially if you are not clear), study, review, test—next! When you are a student, there are teachers everywhere.

If you are a student now, you will be committed to being a student for the remainder of your life. This is the wisest position to fill and the most important role to accept. As a student, you are positioned to learn from everything—the splinter, the hot stove, the rapid descent, the unkind word, the shunning by a group not your own, the preciousness of life and how quickly it lets go. As a student, when you look at a flower, you see it was once a seed and that it will likely plant itself again; you see the earth; you see the birds that sow seeds afar and the insects that work both for and against that single flower. To a student, a flower is so much more than simply a flower. It is first a stand for beauty. It is a world containing so many elements, roles, and occupations—just like you.

> *"If you are a student, such is the richness of your sight. An investment in knowledge pays the best interest."*
>
> —Benjamin Franklin

I used Franklin's quote as a thoughtful impetus (part of my focus phrase process, contemplating a single phrase for a certain period of time and then writing about it) on a particular day. Investment is the word that played out throughout the day, and I asked myself this question: "What is this activity an investment in?" I applied that question to virtually every action. I consistently eliminate actions that invest, ultimately, in things that do not matter to me, that have no relevance to the priorities of my life.

Since I had a heightened awareness of adding knowledge to my core, I evaluated the library books I had on hand. I measured my available time and decided research reading for my next book would not pay as many immediate dividends as reading on my current health issues. A trip to the library to return those books was added to the menu of the day—and a book on the relationship of food to healing was placed on interlibrary order. Three other books came home with me, and I invested an hour in reading a book relating principles of Chinese energy medicine to eating patterns. It produced immediate behavioral changes and quite a few "aha" discoveries. Thanks, Benjamin, you old scoundrel. Contemplating one of his wise sayings throughout my day produced some measurable, positive results. The philosophers of old were right—we do become what we most think about.

What If I Just Acted Like Everything Was Easy?

"Blessed are those who dream dreams and are
willing to pay the price to make them come true."

—Henry Viscardi Jr.

"Pay the price" is bootstrap-pulling-up thinking. If it's good and worthy, it must also come with a cost. A dream is true simply by being dreamt. A dream comes to trueness the instant I am willing for it to be true; simple, not complex. "What if I just pretended like everything was easy?"

Then it would be.

Dreams and anxiety focusing around their potential price tags belong in the darkness. Anxiety that keeps a dream from taking a step forward is like a rogue engineer pointing out every potential disaster waiting to happen. Dreams becoming real and possible belong in the lightness of our ease. Engineers are essential, just not in every phase of a project!

Smart and technologically literate are two different things. I contributed to the effort to encourage my friend to get a specific mobile device. And now he views me as his resident phone specialist. I had to train for an hour with a technology specialist before I even got my own device. He called recently, so frustrated, saying "I have tried everything," and then he provided a long list of all those attempts, "and I can't get my volume up so I can hear my phone ring. Help!" I headed to his office, where he promptly put the device in my hand. I reflected just for a moment on this peculiar turn of events. I, who just recently pledged to stop declaring that I was technically challenged and who marched over the water on a ferry once a week for months in order to be trained in the fundamentals of keyboard functions, was seen as a competent source of assistance for someone else's technology challenge. It was an amazing turn of events. So, phone in hand, I asked myself, "What was the first question my favorite computer geek always asked me?" The answer was immediate because it was always the same first question. "Is it plugged in?" I looked, wondering, is the ringer turned on? No, it wasn't. I turned the phone face up in my friend's hands, and without judgment and with complete empathy, I said, "This first little button here is often accidentally toggled. When you turn the sound on—see?—it gives you both the visual indicator and—feel that?—it's set to vibrate as well. Same when you turn it off." He accepted the simplicity of the solution as his own critical judge. He groaned, "How could I have not known?" He chastised himself out loud.

I knew perfectly well the answer to his "How?" New skill sets by their very newness don't allow for ease of use. Through discovery and practice, we begin to adopt a thing so thoroughly that it becomes second nature. In the space of not knowing, we also tend to believe solutions are complex. Frequently, they are simple. I still often jump into a solution matrix that is complicated and confounding. And I then have to work my way back to simplicity.

My computer language is growing daily. Abilities build upon themselves. One of the most important things is to support my learning with context, which some people call linguistic framing. I stopped saying, "I'm technologically challenged," and replaced it with, "I am committed to increasing my computer skills." What a difference one sentence has made in my experience.

***

You are so smart. Try saying that to yourself for a few days. And then ask yourself, "What if I just pretended everything was easy?"

***

I set aside the drama from the trauma. "How could I not have known?" doesn't serve learning as much as asking, "How can I apply this to the next time something like this happens?" Difficult conversations have their own basic challenges without adding the festoonery of drama. If I see these many challenges as bull's-eyes in a game of darts, I can approach each one with equal verve. If it were "easy," I would just play—dispatch the dart after some aim. I would not agonize over it and turn it over and over in my hand and speculate on potential outcomes. I would just throw the dart. I tell myself, "Start starting." It would be just that easy with the events of my life—walking in a cadence that is consistent, manageable, and even playful. There is really no pretending here—it can be just that easy. And on the days that it isn't, I pretend!

Every Road's an Adventure When You Travel with Enthusiasm

Every road is an adventure. Even for a metaphorical thinker, on this specific day, this was literally true. I drove into San Francisco on a summer Saturday. Park Presidio Boulevard was filled with people. Most people had guidebooks and questioning, puzzled looks. I enjoyed vicarious discovery while proceeding precisely where my GPS directed me, to my friend's house. I traveled streets and a road quintessentially San Francisco: a vertical climb virtually observing the oncoming view—the view was just all hill. I was reminded of the correct way to position my tires on such a steep grade, and, before I knew it, I was off on another adventure with my friend. Turns out a "shortcut" through Golden Gate Park was no shortcut at all. The streets were closed for an event, but the detours created an adventure, which I enjoyed very much. I embraced the new and unanticipated views with enthusiasm. Some people say I was lost for a time. I say I took some time for adventuring.

A Fine Role Model for Enthusiasm and Learning

In the company of a rat terrier named Webster, I see the epitome of enthusiasm and learning. He is willing to learn just about anything I have the patience and consistency to teach him. And the breadth of things that generate an enthusiastic response from him, from a knock at the door to a drive across the country, are just amazing. This paean of praise for dogs could go just about anywhere in this book—I think it belongs here!

In Praise of Dogs

Dogs: they are the best parts of most experiences, the companion I long for when two-legged companions offer betrayal. Dogs are the softest crying cloth, the ever-present comfort on four legs (sometimes less than four legs!) delivering dedication with no sense of obligation or beholding. Dogs: pure enthusiasm. Unreserved excitement for the most dependably simple things. The most certain confidence keeper. The wisest barometer and thermometer. The most attentive nurse, skilled diagnostician, and best pillow. Dogs: a reason to rise from the reading or writing that has dominated the day and walk. An invitation to see and understand without words: learning a different kind of language. A study in compassionate service and unconditional loyalty, loyalty within clear limits because sometimes a piece of bacon wins over even our strongest ties. Dogs: the foundation of unembarrassed confessions of affection. Because you can always call someone you love, it is the dog you most miss while on a journey away from home. Dog hair. The added bonus on every dinner plate—a dog's hair adds an alchemical element. Dog hair leaves the house on every guest's clothing—no fanfare required. You're welcome. Unfettered love is tucked into everything in the house: the flying fur is just the icon, the metaphor. Of course dog is G-o-d spelled backward. Of course it is.

Chapter 10

Relationship
Appreciate Your Friends

"Joy and gratitude come from
belonging to a community."

—Pam Matchie-Thiede

H ealthy relationships support the ability to give and receive. We are better when we can move together, pull together, and be together. We are meant to be in community. For all the focus on individualism, it is simply not possible to survive as long or as well on our own.

I live in the North Country, where in winter a single snowfall can exceed a foot. Alone, you may not be able to clear your own driveway and may find yourself stuck at home without the services of taxpayer-funded snowplows. When community members chip in, one plow and one driver can help so many. Kind neighbors often show up with snowblowers and shovels, ready to whisk away the snow that is an overwhelming barrier for only one person. If you have been the recipient of such a kindness, you understand how gratitude feels at minus ten degrees.

The movie *Pay It Forward* showed the personal joy that buoys us when, after receiving help, we get the opportunity to satisfy another person's need. The idea became a popular movement when the movie was released in 2000 and is now experiencing a resurgence, with diners anonymously picking up the tab for utter strangers and other acts of generosity. Our life experiences happen in waves and cycles. Things go well for a while—until they don't. Then, what was easy before becomes hard, even insurmountable, and we need help. If we're lucky enough, we have friends to call on. Sometimes the friends even see our need before we ask and reach out to give us a hand. These friends are also our community.

When my mother died, I'd been staying with her, four hours from my home. Knowing that when she passed, our house would be a gathering place for relatives, a friend blessed me by cleaning my home of the dirt, hair, and clutter from two dogs, three cats, and five humans that had accumulated when I was unable to handle these tasks as we managed her long, fatal illness. Twenty years later, I still remember the depth of that kindness with increasing tenderness. She stepped forward and helped me in a way I will never forget.

Sharing in community and trusting relationships transforms us. Giving without expecting to receive anything in return brings us wealth beyond any monetary currency. It connects us with the riches of our inner goodness, expanding the size of the pie so there is always enough for everyone—and who doesn't love pie?

—Pam Matchie-Thiede

Alone into Together

I consider my solitude as I sit outside. The waters of Puget Sound are at a minus tide, revealing so plainly why the expanse in front of me is called "Useless Bay." People stroll to the tide's edge at low tide, and there's no hope for a boat moored close to shore in this bay; hence, the "useless" part of the name. The whirring throaty buzz of hummingbirds comes from the feeder to my left. The songbirds are rehearsing their liturgy, and a sound like fast-moving sandpaper blocks striking each other, squeaky and intermittent, comes from the crows in the trees. There are eagles so close I can appreciate the majesty of their white hoods even without my helpful eyeglasses.

I sit soaking in this rare demonstration of Pacific Northwest spring sun. My better judgment reminds me I have more artwork to complete. Oh, yeah; this is just a pause in the day. It is a contribution to my vitamin D3 intake and an investment in my relationship to myself. The crow crowd (I don't call them a "murder" here) wonders if my presence means food will soon be thrown to them. They cannot imagine any other reason I would be outside, simply sitting on the deck. I do exist only to feed them, don't I?

I said to a friend that rest and friends are two of the most important things in our lives…and yet in our busy-ness, we often place both elements last in our day—if we manage to place them in our day at all. Aware that I have just invested in that first part of the equation—rest—I pick up my phone and call several of my cherished souls whose voices I haven't heard in a bit. Laughter and stories punctuate the birdsong. There was the second part: friends. This equation and the balance between the two are what it is to be content in a party of one. And this ease in my own company, my own "party of one" creates a way for contentment to be present in my larger circle of relationship.

Inevitably, I will dine alone when I travel. Over the years I've come to appreciate the unique opportunity that taking a meal by myself offers me. A dependable part of this experience is how restaurant staff relate to a single diner. "Just one?" they often inquire, or "A party of—one?" I've come to the habit of laughingly giving this reply: "There's no 'just' about it. Yes, a party of one, and what a party it is!"

Fully Present for Yourself First

Like the children's literature creature going from one animal to another asking, "Are you my mother?" I have been searching for a sense of home all my life. In relationships outside my blood family, in places, in shiny shells set up with colorful walls and complementary furniture. In spite of the fact that I have written, "When I say I am going home, I mean I am going where you are," the hard and contradictory truth is, "I am my own home."

Home is an answer of place from deep within me. Recently, in the face of a loving but frustrated litany of, "Here's what's not quite right about you," I've recognized that someone else's assessment of me is not a depressing truth. It's just their truth. In spite of having been paired in marriage and added into the lives of many cherished friends, I really am one, alone at the end of any of these relational equations. I have an incredibly supportive circle. Increasingly, while I honor the spiritual value of friendship and intimate relationships, I must acknowledge I enter my dreams alone, I walk the halls of my nightmare fears alone, and I press forward into growth and understanding, acceptance and personhood, alone. "A party of one": yes, indeed, and what a party it is. Being attentive to that single party first and before others is what enables me to be in dynamic relationship with others. I take care of myself, first. Then I am confident I am able to give, from wholeness and fullness, to my larger circle.

Being Attentive Has So Many Rewards

Years ago, I observed, "The call to serve takes many forms in the life of a compassionate heart." Listen better and be more respectful toward yourself, and you will be more respectful and celebratory of the stories your friends tell. They are telling them for a reason— especially if it's the seventh time they are telling them! If a friend says something shocking, like wanting to "punch someone," withhold your judgment. Instead of correcting them or offering your alternative action, try inquiry, "Why?" Or observation, "Oh, you feel like punching them, eh?" Just as some pharmaceuticals act to potentiate other drugs, so do we serve that function in our friendships. A friend takes what is already working and helps raise it up a notch or two. In this model, being attentive to your relationship to yourself allows the same sort of capacity to dial up what is working within you. I remind myself of this truth as often as I remind my circle of friends: Tending to our own needs first is the finest way to be in service to each other. Compassionate service often looks a lot like being attentive to personal needs.

A Lingering Scent

Perhaps I haven't known you since I was five. I've known you just a small bit of the time I've been alive, and yet you are a part of all I say and do, present to all my joys and witness to the things that are hard. You are my friend.

We've not been singing together since we were ten. And yet I can't think of a time recently that there's been a better companion, a stronger show, a sweeter harmony line sung just below the gentle melody that you and I have come to know.

Not part of my childhood, yet instrumental to my growth, you have been elemental in the depth of all my knowing. Your friendship and your wisdom shared so deeply and so strong has given me fortitude on the best of days as well as those days when things go so keenly wrong. I haven't known you since I was a child, and yet our cadence and trust in current days reflects a compressed lifetime, a distilled essence that has the lingering fragrance of the most timeless perfume. New friends complete the circle of lifelong friends. If you are fortunate enough to have even one good friend, you really do hold the hand of the world.

Stand by Your Family

When I was almost six, I grasped that Mother's Day meant doing something really special and significant for your mother. How very much I wanted to be grown-up and do the right thing on a holiday. I gathered the pennies that my family provided me when I did something of value around the house. I think I had a double fistful, which must have been just shy of fifty cents. It felt like a treasure chest full of money to me! Happily, I slipped out of the house and, like a very big girl, walked the two and a half blocks to Tooze Florist on Stark Street. I reached up, piled my riches on the counter, and proudly announced, "I'm here to get something wonderful for my mother for Mother's Day." Only decades later did I come to understand the pressures piled on a flower business the Friday before Mother's Day—the most demanding day in a florist's entire year!

It was a balding man who smiled and scooped up my pile of money. He asked me what exactly did I want? I surveyed the large store. Corsages! My sister, Judy, had given ladies at her wedding corsages. That must be a really cool thing. If it was good for a once-in-a-lifetime wedding, it'd be good for a mother's holiday. Proud of my decision, I announced, "A corsage." He gave me the choice of having it delivered or waiting while he made it. The immediate satisfaction of gift-giving has been with me a very long time. "Now!" I said, reasoning, *Why wait until Sunday when she could have it now? All the more days to enjoy it.* That dear man stopped what he was doing and made a glorious, very large corsage. He placed it in a big waxed bag. It rested on the end of a large fern. He folded over the edge and put a large pin through the end of the bag. Wow. I watched his every move with fascination. It was the most beautiful thing I'd been involved with in my young life. After he placed the corsage in my hand, he gave me a dime. He told me I'd overpaid him. Of course, I believed him, since I'd hauled two fistfuls of coin in there. I had no idea of the enormity of the compassionate generosity I'd just received.

My profoundly earnest effort was not met with the anticipated joy. After I festively, dancingly presented my Happy Mother's Day present, I was heatedly questioned and was promptly walloped. My mother was horrified. She understood the cost of what she held in her hand, and she was convinced I had to have stolen it from the local flower shop. Reasoning that I was not inclined toward theft carried no impact.

"I bought it with my own money. Really." I even produced the dime change to prove that I had more than enough to purchase this honor for her on Mother's Day. Her horror gave way to embarrassment. She filled in the generous corners of the story. A grabbed coat; the hat donned; the purse retrieved from its spot. My mother snagged my hand, and I was dragged at a rapid clip to the flower shop. I greeted the bald man like the old and dear friend he had so recently become. My mother, however, addressed him by name.

Wow, she knows everybody, I thought. They spoke in whispered tones. It escalated into what I recognized as a restrained argument. The was a lot of headshaking and no-saying on both their parts. I saw that my mother finally made some kind of purchase, because she pulled money out of her wallet. I guessed at that point that she must have taken the delivery option, because, unlike me, she walked out of the store with nothing of beauty in her hand—just my hand, firmly grasped. The walk back home was not nearly as fast as the first part of this endeavor. She was softer on the way home. After she hung up her coat and put away her hat, she had a little talk with me. The particulars elude me now. I suspect they eluded me then, too. I can only guess that it was about the true value of money and learning my lesson. I do remember the word "embarrassment" figured in somewhere. And I remember that she did thank me for my gift.

My own experience as a young girl with money and the miracles that come from the compassionate kindness of strangers shaped my attitude toward family and gifting. The joy for me isn't so much in the response of the receiver. It's in that first impulse of longing to create a gift for another. It is from that place that the gift gets given back in so many unexpected ways. That "giveback" is like the dime I held in the palm of my hand as a sincere child.

The other thing I know now that I didn't know then is that my mother did carry a thing of beauty in her hand back home: me.

Whether she saw it or not, my action was based in true intent and honest affection. There's beauty in that, even when it's not recognized.

***

We listen. We listen. We move. We sit. It rains. The sun comes out. There stands a friend. We listen. We laugh. We share. We sit. We move. It rains. There stands a friend. We listen. We share. We sit. We move. The sun comes up. There. I stand a friend.

No Day Is Wasted in Which a Single Moment Is Spent on Love

No lacy red hearts; just encouragement, support, and living to the edge of myself. Truth telling is love, and so are holding your tongue, listening hard, accepting responsibility, remaining quiet, and holding onto a new story in order to hear, for the second time, someone else's story. Looking and holding a glance. Touching an elbow while wordlessly walking past, willingly and joyfully accepting a cup of tea or coffee. Cooking dinner as well as cleaning the dishes. Love is both uncompromising and making compromise. Love dresses as the grandest of contradictions and wears colorful garments made with asymmetrical balance.

If You Have One Friend, You Hold the Hand of the World

"Friendship is the only cement that will ever hold the world together."

—Woodrow Wilson

A scene from *Tombstone* with Val Kilmer portraying Doc Holliday remains vivid in my memory. Doc's hauled himself off his deathbed to help a group of men defend his friend, Wyatt Earp. The defenders were shocked to see him. They thought he should be in bed, and they questioned him:

"Whad'ya doin' here?"

"Wyatt's my friend."

One of the guys said, "Hey, I got a lot of friends."

After a pause, Doc said simply, "I don't."

***

We are all connected. Two friends contacted me today asking for prayerful support. And two other friends called me today telling me they were praying for my health. Those were "old" friends, people woven long into my history. A friend called me to explore a possibility of mutual benefit. We discussed the opportunity and ultimately decided no was the best answer.

All day long, my friends filled in, like mortar between the building bricks of my events and experiences. One greets another through me. Our shared connections bond us exponentially. Yes, in a large view, relationships/friendships do hold the world together. In the micro perspective, my up-close worldview, my friends, in many instances, hold me together.

We hold you close, with open hands, to help you stand strong. We hold you close, with hands clasped in prayer, that you will stand tall. Whether you are near or far…you are ever embraced in our hearts and prayers. Remembering our naming and embracing a new name by remembering the old one… To remember…embrace your love and hold her hand and whisper how precious, how precious your breath. To remember, honor your friend and set aside the indulgence of regret. Extend your hand now and rest your arm on the strength of your choices.

To remember…rise a little earlier and wrap your intuition around the world. To remember…gift a stranger, support an aching heart with anonymous care, walk more gently, and thank the roots of your favorite tree for all their work.

To remember…shout the anger of loss down the canyons of mystery and open your arms, ready, for the next birth in which they will assist. Light a candle…bridge the miles of stupefying loss and know that only little graces, little stones, rebuild the sanctuary which we know as hope. And this sanctuary becomes, again, the shelter for many unspoken sobs. In that shelter there is safety and protected healing.

Light a candle to remember and then sleep. Deeply sleep. When you awaken, the world awaits your next loving song. Because of the strength of your remembering and the profound love with which you hold your friend—you will continue to sing.

Be Certain

You must know I am your friend. Be certain of that.

I accept you as you are. I see you for who you are—really.

I notice all your real you-ness when you think no one is looking. What I see is awesome, amazing, inspiring.

I know you have big dreams and wonder how you will ever do it all. And yet, you answer that question every day. In all your little things lies your answer; the way you simply show up to life, every day… Bravely. In spite of your reservations. With your arms open wide.

Open arms engaged in a circle of giving and receiving and passing along.

You have passed so many gifts my way—there is one that is endlessly treasured: You! You are a gift I enjoy every day.

***

When I was nineteen years old, I was the switchboard operator for a college in San Francisco. One of the professors noticed that I was often writing when I wasn't occupied answering the incoming calls or greeting guests. One day, he asked me, "What are you always writing?" I told him that largely, I was writing poetry. He gave a considered pause and then asked me if I could write a book of poetry about any subject—what would I write about? I answered without hesitation that I would write a book about friendship. I am certain that I am alive today because of the good friends I have had throughout my life. And my poetry about such friends comes quickly to me.

A Feather

I found a feather in my path.
I knew not what it meant.
Was it an Angelic messenger's
"something" that was sent?
Or was it simply a bird in flight
whose weary wing was spent?
To see this feather as I walk
reminds me of my friend.
We see signs in everything

from our dawn to our day's end.
There are those who say that
those lines we draw are made too straight—
never meant to bow or bend.
When I find a feather there...
Reminding me of this walk of grace...
it doesn't matter where I see it
it just matters that it is true...
Whenever I see a feather alight
I think about and pray for you.

Chapter 11

Leadership
Lead and Follow a Leader

"Our best depends on us. Together."

—Dr. Kymn Harvin

O ur collective wisdom—both as leaders and followers—is wanted, longed for, needed. People look to us in breath-holding, breath-taking, breath-honoring ways. Let us give them what they want most: our best, so they can be their best.

Our best depends on our willingness to Stop. Quiet. Listen. Receive. Give.

Our best depends on soulfulness…the art of living and leading and following from the ocean floor instead of the choppy surface.

Our best depends on knowing the people counting on us are both divine and human…just like us.

—Dr. Kymn Rutigliano

"And" Instead of "Or"

When I added this to my original poem it first read "lead *or* follow a leader." It didn't take me long to realize that this was not what I believed about real leadership. I changed the sentence to lead and follow a leader. That is what is true for me. There are examples of leaders who celebrate their own leadership by asserting that there is no one they can follow, that they believe they have all the information and answers they need and they are their own best advisors. While their case may seem compelling at first, it turns out that leaders actually do need to know how to follow.

Talk to People Who Know How to Lead and Follow

When I am at my best in a leadership position, I am leader and follower, leader and learner. I lead by allowing others to learn to lead. One of the oddest places to learn about leadership is in training my dogs. This kind of training has transferable applications. This one adventurous, curious rat terrier had the habit of door dashing with visitors. A guest at the door? *Out* Webster would go. My first impulse was terror and worry. He was not familiar with cars and roads. Gripped by concern, I would yell, "Nooooooo, come back…" and eventually, he would.

I hung out with a mother who had three children under six years of age and noticed how misbehavior could be otherwise directed. She'd toss fun things. Make a joke. Pretend to be having a great deal of fun. The next time Webster door dashed, I applied what I'd learned. I grabbed some just-cooked chicken out of the fridge. I loudly emphasized, using a familiar word, "Look at this treat. I'm going over here with this treat. Yum. This treat looks like fun!!!!" Webster was at my side in seconds, ready for something delicious. And I understood that my anxiety and yelling only made him stay away longer. Who wants to come when they know they are just going to be yelled at? However, an invitation to come for fun is a different matter altogether. And then? I got to work training myself for a different protocol when inviting guests into my home! Learn and lead.

Leadership Has a Long Reach

There comes a time when the answers you provide your own questioning heart are more significant than the equations, methods, or assertions of others. Big people protect little ones. Those who have a voice speak up for those who cannot speak for themselves. Those who have been helped, help others. We live in a circle, not on a line. Leadership, good leadership, could be drawn as the never-ending circle. Leading and following become the pixels that make up the line that draws the circle: leaders investing in future leaders and leaders investing in their own future by learning as they also lead.

Let me introduce you to one of my favorite leaders. The first time Robbie walked into one of my stores, everybody there was drawn to him. Heads turned. Several staff members wanted to wait on Robbie. I noticed that about him on the campus at Willamette University. Essentially, people near him asked, "Who is that guy, and where is he going?" They wanted to go, too. He never had to invite people to do what he was doing. He was having so much fun on the way that people just wanted to join in with whatever he was doing. I knew that playfulness and fun would be key elements in his developing leadership style. Real leaders are very clear regarding how to be an able follower.

I asked Robbie about the roots of his unique leadership style. I wondered how he saw them emerging out of the experiences of his life. This is what he told me.

"I was aware that I had leadership skills. At the beginning, I was that annoying child who just couldn't stop asking questions. I was just naturally that inquisitive. I have a unique way of sincerely asking questions because I want to learn from people. In every interview I've had for any job, this is something that really stands out to the people who are considering hiring me and who I am considering working for.

"Asking questions is tricky—when you ask a tenured person who feels proprietary about what they know, they can resist or wonder why you are asking, especially if it's something they think you should already know. But in fact, I am interested even if it is a process with which I am very familiar. I want to know how they came to the process, how they learned it, what they think of it. But the questions can make some people uncomfortable, that is, until they understand why I am asking. I want to know how and why they've come to the answer. I'm not looking for agreement or alignment alone, I'm looking for perspective and process. Those two things are more important at times…to understand how they got to a specific outcome. It helps me learn how they learn. And that helps me be a better leader for them."

Expressing appreciation is a significant element of Robbie's leadership style. I asked him about that. He explained:

"The top components of my leadership style are appreciation, loyalty, the ability to learn, taking away the sense of shame around failure, and contextualizing failures as learning opportunities. It is still a little bit organic, but I work toward defining it so I can better teach it. I have the opportunity to address newly graduated business students who are building their leadership portfolios and launching into the work world. It really excites me to be able to embody a functional demonstration for those who are a generation behind me that what used to be considered "soft" skills are actually the most significant skills of a dynamic leader.

"My leadership style emerged out of the intentions I have for my own life. I want to bring out the best in people. Caring about them, finding out what motivates them. I do believe that people show up to their jobs really wanting to do their best. Largely nobody consciously begins their day saying, 'I want to show up for work today and be miserable and make others miserable. I want to hate what I'm doing and make things awful for my team.' I don't think that many people choose that attitude on purpose. Everybody has off days. As I work to understand a team and begin to see what brings them satisfaction in their job—those off days become fewer and further between."

I asked Robbie how he keeps his knowing of the motivating factors of each team member from becoming manipulative. He explained:

"Yes, there are those who teach that finding out what incentives will motivate each person can be used as leverage in order to extract maximum performance value from them. Get buy-in now so we can get high performance out of them later.

"There's attrition in every employment circumstance. The team that I am leading now is going to be different in six months, in a year, in two years. Whether I'll move on, they'll move on, or new people will be added, the dynamic of the team is going to change. I never let that influence how I'm inspiring the team or what I'm learning from them, whether they go on to lead other groups or stay. I take great pride in the fact I've heard from recruiters over the years that they can tell that the person they've just placed in a leadership position demonstrates such outstanding skills, that they are pleased to hear about the training they've received from me and were provided by me to become an inspiring leader. I develop team members to be contributing partners in any group dynamic, whether it's my group or someone else's. I invest in the person, not just the company objectives. The person comes first, the company's objectives come second.

"The ethical commitment that I have to building people up as human beings is at the root of all I do. And, like roots, that's not the thing that is evident. What *is* visible is that I create teams of people who learn to work cohesively, who set aside gossip, who support each other's efforts at learning, who actually look forward to coming to work because it's fun and rewarding. Those are the elements in my tree, to use your metaphor, that are visible.

"I contribute to the world, the larger world, by planting seeds of excellent leadership in the people. I invest openhandedly in the people, knowing that I will ultimately be contributing to both the success of the company I am working for *and* the community in which we all live.

"Something comes to mind from when I took a new position and was in introductory interviews. I hadn't even had a formal workday yet. Some executives offered to fire two 'problem' people before I even started my job. They explained that these workers had been problem employees for a long time and that they thought they might be paving a way for my success if they got rid of them for me. I chuckled. I declined and said that if they'd been there so long, maybe they just hadn't had the opportunity to work with someone who could inspire them to behave differently. Then one of the interviewers chuckled, too. And he told me that response is probably the best possible thing I could have said—to invest in them as people, not as 'problematic employees.' Once people understand that I truly care for them, believe in them, and want to provide resources to them…*that* is when they start performing better for the business."

Since he demonstrates a fairly altruistic view toward leadership, I wanted to know what Robbie's reward was for being this kind of leader. His answer didn't come as a surprise.

"Seeing when people thrive, when they can pull off some amazing wins, or when there is a noticeable difference in their family and their community and the other things that they are serving in outside of work…and I get to hear about that and witness it, that's the reward for me. This is why I like locally based businesses. Maybe ultimately we are all changing the world, but we're doing it beginning with our community first.

It's like asking a gardener why they are doing stuff for their garden in the middle of the cold, uncomfortable winter. Nothing is growing, and yet they are still tending their garden. A gardener knows that even when growth isn't evident, there are things that must be done in the off-season. Then there is growth and harvest and measurable outcomes that are visible and worth celebrating."

We Are Made of Stars

It was a remarkable period of time when Commander Chris Hadfield was addressing those who listened from the International Space Station. Philosophical and educational in his outreach, he made living among the stars seem closer to our days. He and his fellow astronauts inspired this reflection: how does this earth-footed being comprehend the impulse to sit among the stars? There is a longing to shine among them, as if a part of my heart was long ago folded into their heat and light. Our nexus is understood in that stars are made by the sum of other parts—as am I. And, like a star, I shine not because of how I am shaped but because of my intention. I shine by virtue of the intention of which I am made.

A Parade Named You

You walk people to places they never imagined that they would stand.

You stand with them.

You walk people to places that they hoped to go—but could not visualize the way.

Once there, you stand with them and expand their view even more. You are an excellent vehicle: an inviter, one who draws from before and entices, one who coaches from behind and inspires.

Shoulder to shoulder, you expend camaraderie, profound humor, and shared vision. What an honor to march in a parade that will always be remembered as you.

Chapter 12

Dream
Do What You Love

"The space will open for you to do what you love when you believe that what you love is worth doing."

—Sue Robson

I t is essential for me to be willing to ask myself often: are the things I am doing, or the choices I am making, taking me in the direction of my dream, of that which I love to do? Are they taking me toward what matters most to me? Am I willing to identify the changes that need to be made so I can do what I love? I cannot just dream or vision what I want for my life and keep doing what I am doing, especially if what I am doing is not getting me to where I want to go. I must speak frequently about what I love to do, write it down on cards, and state it as if it were true right now. It takes courage to do what I love. It means going after what I want when those closest to me may not follow. It means brushing away the chatter of the past voices telling me to do the safe or logical thing.

I am a coach, a workshop facilitator, and a writer. I love doing this work. I love being on the edge with others, uncovering what is important and stepping into what matters deep in our bones. It rocks my world and ignites an energy that warms the room and brings an aliveness to me and those I am with. And yet, I also work in the corporate world. I do both because what I love, my dream, needs to be expressed and it is worth doing. A little over eight years ago, my mom brainstormed with me as to how I could package a workshop to teach others about making and using prayer malas as a spiritual practice. This dream grew from making malas for myself and friends, to a website, writing an instruction booklet, creating kits that have everything one needs to make their own prayer mala, and taking my workshop on the road to locations along the Northern California and Southern Oregon coast. I am in the process of writing my book about this journey. My mom also encouraged me in my lifelong dream to one day live in a home by the ocean. She sent me a book on financial planning and pictures of houses by the water. She never got to see the home I purchased on the Oregon coast, but it is truly a tribute to her and the faith she had in me that if I believed in what I was doing, I could do anything. And so I did.

—Sue Robson

May Your Heart Be Awakened to All Your Dreams

"It takes a lot of courage to show your dreams to someone else."

—Irma Bombeck

Show Your Dreams to the World. Willingness: just be willing to see, observe, consider. The opposite of a closed mind is willingness. An awakened heart does not mean the heart embraces everything; it means that it is awake to everything and intentionally chooses what it will encircle. Being awakened to my dreams simply expands my sense of options and possibility at every juncture. I've been showing my dreams to the world in my writing for a good portion of my life. I share my dreams in my social networks. I write them on whiteboards and on my walls. It strikes me that people think courage is required to speak your dreams because someone might belittle them or minimize the dream when it is shown. I can be grateful for early childhood education in how to manage dream minimization. I learned early how to respond to "You can't do that." Why argue? Just do it. Then let them be surprised when they are invited to the celebration.

Pursue What You Love

I remember gymnastics and the feeling of dismounting the horse. I knew when every motion had been in perfect succession and I had "nailed it." So it is with one's craft—any craft. My experience is with the craft of writing. On some rare days, I get it right the first time: precision as I leave the pommel horse of my work. It happens periodically, the transcendent moment when craft transports a creative person to a holy place, a place of sacred athleticism. It is a place where silence and sound meet, where engaging with art becomes a physical exertion. It is an exercise in inspiration. It is exhilarating and exhausting.

A writer writes: every day. It is the work, the practice of the craft. Edit. Sculpt phrases. Cross out words. Replace words or eliminate them. Hold sentences to the light, turn them, confirm balance. When the words sparkle, put them back and move on. That is the work, consistently. Hemingway acknowledged the everydayness of good writing by confessing that in general, out of thousands of words in a day, a writer is bound to seize upon fifty good ones. And so it goes, most of the time.

Those "everyday" days pave the road on the journey for the luminous moment—that moment when experience agrees with immediacy and they inform the spirit of any permission ever granted toward grace. And they work in synergistic, committed cadence to produce something extraordinary. That is the incandescent crossroad on the journey. The markers and signs read anew as the road of creating moves on. The trick is to embrace the ordinary, lovingly, each day, on its own dependable merit. Each mile on the road is indeed drawing closer to another brilliant intersection (as the ordinary invites the extraordinary). There is more road than crossroad, and one cannot be held in higher esteem over the other. They are inseparable. Lucidity has varying measures of shine, and each day spent pursuing the passion of craft is brilliant in its own way.

What Art Does

A different collection of luminaries every year is featured in the Kennedy Center Honors ceremony. I like to watch one awards show each year. This one acknowledges with full national force the significant role that the arts play in the life of America. I put away the work of my day. I turn off my phone. For two hours, I am transported. Commercial breaks become an opportunity to reflect on how each craft, each person honored had a place of significance in my history. Art engages. It draws you in. It's the train wreck you have to watch, and it's the prolonged note, the beauty of which pulls across the skin of your life like a knife and draws blood. *Art*: It's not the neat and the orderly. It can be uncomfortable. It is the inspiring and the impacting. It's immediate. Dangerous. And essential. As Bruce Springsteen's music ran its full brush across the palette of the evening, I see it again and again—the art of America stirring the soul. I saw the memories playing on the screens of every person in attendance there at the Kennedy Center, both in my home and other homes within the broadcast reach. One year, particularly, I recall Bruce Springsteen's lyrical presence, which like Whitman, like Angelou, uniquely calls out that which is undeniably American in our experience. The audience was dancing. They were clapping. They could not remain still. They, we, were calling to mind that which once was. That's what art does. It calls to mind that which was before and brings it alive again in this moment, in a way that is neither predictable nor anticipated but wild and utterly breath-stealing. And art makes the future seem more possible and more beautiful. After watching that musical icon and his visceral engagement with his work, I cried. I dried my tears, uttered a holy expletive under my breath, and declined sleep for a bit. I told myself, "You have to write."

I am compelled. Because that is what art does. Leverage the opportunities that work for you: pave the way and seize the clear opportunity regardless of where you are. When I am aligned with passion and right action, questions of self-knowing fall away. "Who am I?" and "What is my dream?" are answered in the authentic impulses that punctuate my days. Clarity visits and leaves no footprints, only dreams. It is a precious, inspired homecoming to return to my dreams after being long away from them.

You Go Where Your Thoughts Go

"A man's life is what his thoughts make of it."

—Marcus Aurelius

Did my father consciously base his driving lessons on the principles of Marcus Aurelius? My first driving lesson occurred down the road. A farmer was laying in his rows for field planting. My dad had me stand and watch the tractor drive from one end of the field to the other.

"I thought you said I was getting a driving lesson?"

"You are."

"I'm going to learn how to drive on a tractor?"

"Just watch."

At each end of the farmer's field were flimsy row markers. As he finished a row, he ran each marker over with his tractor. All this was unfamiliar to me, so I equated the markers to signs, signs that had some ongoing purpose, and I commented to my dad how weird it was that he was running over the things that he had apparently so purposefully set.

"He doesn't need them anymore."

"Why?"

"Just watch. You'll figure it out."

After a while I stopped looking at the tractor and observed the farmer instead. After several more rows, I saw what my dad wanted me to see. The driver never took his eyes off the row markers. He didn't look at us, his house, or anything else. He left behind him straight, perfectly measured rows. When we walked out of the field and all the way back to the house, we talked about how driving a car was just like that. When you drive looking immediately in front of you, the vehicle is constantly adjusting, the ride isn't smooth, and turns are abrupt. When you drive with your eyes ahead, focused on the longer view, the path is smooth, the turns are anticipated, and it's a better and safer ride. He showed me the difference between the two ways of looking. Highway 53 is comprised of switchback curves and hairpin turns. When he focused on the road in front of him, I almost got carsick. It was a rocky, shifting ride. When his gaze fell forward along the road, he drove to the "row marker," and the car motored smoothly.

This became a perfect metaphor for me. You naturally move in the direction of what you're looking toward, or, more to the point, you go where your thoughts go. At first, standing in that field, I was certain it was the most unsuitable place in the world to learn how to drive. What do you know? Marcus Aurelius and my dad had a few things in common.

Lean Forward into Your Life

I wonder how many dawns I just poured into the paint palette. Could I explain that to someone? Many people I know who paint don't experience this extraordinary wrestling forth of the work. I know many people think of painting as "craft," or more to the point, "production work." That is not how it is for me. Painting is to me what the sportswriter Walter Wellesy "Red" Smith said writing was for him—all he had to do was open a vein and hold his wrist over the paper. Paint is like that for me; it pours out of my veins. The colors come right out of my soul and mix on the paper. These forms I just painted had my longings and inspiration and breath poured into each stroke, so that when somebody looked at what I'd created, they would feel uplifted, encouraged—supported.

And in that, the art gives back. As with a practiced faith, there's an ethereal reward, but in the immediate, there is a liturgy of my creation. The ritual I must go through to paint is not conventionally recognizable: not incense, but the vapors of my anxiety and anticipation rising. Not prayers, just formless utterings framing the unnamed sounds of my desire to communicate peace, passion, hope. And order. There has to be order before I can make chaos. Ironically, it can take me three days to "ready" a studio space, and less than one hour to mess it up with paint and splatters and painterly towels, with brushes everywhere drying. And there is plenty of space to lean forward. The mess is always worth it!

When You Jump into Your Dreams, Are Your Eyes Open or Closed?

"The jump is so frightening between where I am and where I want to be. Because of all I may become, I will close my eyes and leap."

—Mary Anne Radmacher

When I was a little girl, I would save my money and go to our corner drugstore, which had what I thought was the world's largest collection of greeting cards. And they were for sale! Bliss.

I loved all the images and would take an hour to select one card. Even at eight years old, I thought the inside greetings were just plain silly. I would purchase my card, march home, and use my dad's white strike-out correcting sheet to set those insides right. (Had liquid Wite-Out not yet been invented?) Then it was ready for a personal note and was sent off to some interested family friend or a relative who required a thank-you. I was not sure what "precocious" meant, but after receiving something in the mail from me, folks always told my mother that's what I was.

But my affinity for greeting cards began years earlier. My childhood home had a wrought-iron door with a slot that opened to receive the mail. The sharp, succinct sound of mail dropping could be heard throughout the house. And when there was a series of sounds, I knew there was more than one piece of mail. I might have been three when I began to associate the man in the blue outfit carrying the big, brown leather purse with what I previously thought was the magical appearance of mail. Yes. Even still, I know that association, and something else hasn't changed. I continue to consider mail delivery something of a modern magic trick. For less than the cost of a cup of coffee, I can put three handwritten lines on a piece of paper, and in a matter of hours, that paper will be handed to someone far away from me. I wrote letters to rangers in national parks. I was thrilled when I not only received beautiful information about their particular park, but also that they took the time to include a personal note. My love of all things postal, mail, note-ish, and letterly fostered my dream, one that would begin to express itself soon after I graduated from high school.

In my early twenties, I dreamt of starting my own greeting card company. I would write on the pages of my journal, "I want to be an artist." I longed to create a livelihood that had meaning and use my talents and skills in the service of compelling and inspiring ideas. I was certain that I would have to wait until I was (eh-hem) *really* old, maybe some time in my forties. I thought perhaps by the time I reached the wise age of forty-five, I would have gotten all the education needed and managed to save up enough money to fund my own company.

The rumblings wouldn't leave. I felt unwilling to wait almost twenty years before I could manifest my dream. I wrote to a man who used to own a kite shop in the small community where I lived. He knew a lot about how to make things fly...including one's dreams. I poured my heart out to him in that letter. I told him I realized I didn't know the first thing about operating a business and I barely had a dime to my name. But I knew what I wanted to do. And then I wrote, "The jump is so frightening between where I am and where I want to be. Because of all I may become, I will close my eyes and leap."

I brought the letter to a close and posted it. Soon, a photocopy of that letter came back to me. The jump phrase was circled in red, with his note written in the margin: "THIS sentence, these words, are the reason you are ready to start your business now. You know everything you need to know...and these words should go on one of your first products. If you keep writing stuff like this, you'll have a successful career."

I took his advice. Those words were among the first I crafted in my company. And I've had a career punctuated by many successes.

I have heard stories over the years of how that particular sentence has been the motivation to move people along and give them the courage to put wings to their dreams.

Ha!

Just today, I could fold those words into a letter, whispered after these words, "I am on the cusp of a remarkable journey. All the longings of my life have led me to this amazing transition in my experience."

Ah, yes. Jump.

Many Ways to Jump

Bonnie Rae Nygren tells me that I was one of her first art mentors. This is a privilege that comes with loving to inspire people to connect to and believe in their core creativity. Bonnie Rae inhabited an occupation that fascinated me as a child—and fascinates me still. She worked for the United States Postal Service, spending most of her years as a letter carrier. Her career enabled her to experience what I consider the epitome of living with intention. I am inspired by the story she shares, and she gave me permission to share it with you. Bonnie Rae tells it this way:

"When I began at the USPS, I imagined staying no longer than five years. Five years came and went. On my fifteenth anniversary, I was questioning all of it. What difference am I making? Am I living my best life? I was ready to walk away. Then a miracle happened: Gloria. I met Gloria on my route. After years of sharing our lives in daily conversation and real talk about her illness, I lost her. Cancer took her much too soon, and I was devastated.

"Then my other miracle happened.

"I embraced a new way of seeing my purpose. I sensed that maybe there was another reason for staying. Maybe I could make a difference in a different way. I believe I did far more than deliver mail. I finally let it sink in. It's about who we are, not what we do.

"I started really seeing people and places differently. I stopped thinking the job was supposed to bring me something, and instead, I started wondering what I could bring to the job. I learned names. I asked questions. I cultivated real friendships from the modest seeds of interest. I gave, and in return, received attention. And attention, well…it is everything. Your religion, politics, and culture have made me better. We shared turbulent times in the country, deeply personal losses, and big wins. We are one, when it really matters. Those visits held me together some days. If I came to you broken, I was healed; empty, I was filled; joyful, you found a way to multiply it in ways I couldn't have imagined.

"It's been a laboratory of life: wild success and painful failure—our days, filled with salt and light. The job is just the bones. It's up to us to bring it to life."

Dream Like You Know Where You're Going

It took some amount of negotiating to persuade the young intellectual from Germany to be my guest at that night's performance. We were both guests at the same London bed-and-breakfast, and he had made his very serious views toward life known each morning. While he insisted that musicals were frivolous and a waste of time, he agreed thriftily that not using my second ticket, which I had accidentally purchased, would be a waste of money.

That night both our views toward life shifted. We sat in a West End theater watching Hugo's story line unfold in *Les Misérables*. As the character of Fantine wept over her lost love and life in the song "I Dreamed a Dream," the heart in my guest seemed to be breaking. He was so visibly moved by the spectacle before him and increasingly understood that it was anything but frivolous. Watching this transformation in him, I resolved never to be so achingly in the grasp of a system of rigid assumptions. That musical became my soundtrack for many years. I cannot speak of the standing of that young man's life now, but I know that on that night, he was the first to get to his feet as the curtain signaled the close. With hands above his head, he wept for the wonder. He realized that what he had assumed as frivolous was something else entirely, something powerful and inspiring.

Was it a dream I held for that young man...or simply an accident that I purchased two tickets instead of one? Was I manifesting leadership for his life or just not paying attention? At the end of the matter, the result is answer enough for these questions. As the audience stilled from their wild applause and moved to exit the theater, I was reminded of the wisdom of Mary Anne Evans (a.k.a. George Eliot), who courageously embraced her dream and passion, saying, "It is never too late to become who you might have been." Said another way, "Continue to live toward your dream—the ultimate embrace of it will be worth your journey."

Willingness Shines the Light on Your Path

The young executive spoke at length about her wish to trade her career for full-time mothering, to set aside her career away from home in order to stay home and make a career of raising her three-year-old. As she expressed these sentiments, she burst into tears. I recognized this as a sure way to be certain of our purpose—when just to speak them out loud is so filled with longing that it draws a sob from deep within the belly. Many people tend not to face their longings for this very reason—the discomfort of acknowledging such passion. Instead, they walk along the river with their dreams on the opposite side, only occasionally stealing glances at what they deeply hope.

Let Imagined Outcomes Drive Chosen Actions

He must have been nine. He was tall and slight of build. He was sporting a fleece cape, complete with fancy collar. "Wow," I exclaimed, as he strode past. "It's not every day you meet a superhero." Unsmiling, he nodded, acknowledging the truth of my statement. To confirm, I asked, "Are you really a superhero?" Stoically, he nodded that yes, he was. "Wow, may I have your autograph?" He stared at me. His face registered disbelief at the audacity of my question. With no further hesitation and holding my glance, he replied no. With that, he turned on his tennis-shoed heel and walked away. He mother apologetically shrugged and trudged off behind him. *Hmmm. That is probably a good thing to know*, I thought. *Real superheroes don't give autographs.*

Ribbons of Dreams

We wrap our inspirations, friends, family, loves, aspirations in ribbons of dreams. In so doing we raise our sights, we believe in greater things… Wrap the longings of your heart with these ribbons, and live more courageously, and love more intentionally.

Dream in the Infinite possible; dwell there as often as you can.

Chapter 13

Generosity
Live As If This Is All There Is

"Infinite Players play in complete openness, as in vulnerability. It is not a matter of exposing one's true self that has always been but a way of exposing one's ceaseless growth, the dynamic self that has yet to be."

—James Carse

G enerosity begins within. You cannot give unless you are first transformed. That willingness to be vulnerable is itself an act of courage. Without vulnerability, courageousness is an impossibility.

Once we embrace our generosity, we birth it into the world. The regrets expressed at the end of life are never for the things we were working on, but for the things that we failed to do. I should have…

To live as if this is all that there is means that we accept our mortality. No promise can ever change that. The only promise that we can keep is to be present in every moment, to offer generous service, and to be courageous with the time we have.

Hold time lightly in your hand. Make no promise for tomorrow, for now is all that we possess.

—Robert Ruder

We Cannot Know

If I had known this was my last time in Paris…

My friend laughingly waved her dark chocolate at me, saying, "Maybe if this was going to be the last time I'd ever see you, I'd share this with you." I didn't mean to wring all the funny out of the moment, but the words that immediately poured over my lips were, "How do you know it isn't the last time you'll see me?" We were both stunned into silence from the impact of that single sentence. As outcomes go, this worked out pretty well for me. I got some chocolate, and I have seen her since.

Many years ago, I was offhand in my approach to my visit to Paris. I anticipated that I would return that very fall. I did not. Nor have I in the many autumns that have since come and gone. So few of us have the capacity to sense coming events with accuracy. So each day, what might change if we considered that this might be all there is? I've experienced this in practice while supporting a friend through her battle with several types of cancer at various stages of progression. I've observed how much more easily "I love you" occurs in her conversations. Pointed remarks and truthful observations are delivered with tenderness and absent any apology. I've watched her learn to disavow caring much for the opinions of others in regard to her choices at all levels. The reality of her health has imposed the realization that each day might, indeed, be her last. It's been excellent exercise for the fullness of life stretching before her.

At last tally, it was Cancer: 5, and my friend: 17. On her road to wellness, she's not resorting to taking things for granted. Oh, no. If anything, she is more committed than ever to being fully present to the needs that appear in the day. And it's been part of her lesson to realize that the most important needs to address begin and end with caring for her own health. Such a view has taken practice. And she has taken on the practice much like an athlete preparing for competition.

The Muscle that Builds with Use

"It's a funny thing about life; if you refuse to accept anything but the best, you very often get it."

—W. Somerset Maugham

My friend and former editor, Jan Johnson, also an author and publisher, has a profound capacity to condense truth. She summarizes my thoughts in this way, "Expect the best. Give your best and get the best." In this view, instead of just muscle building, the process is also circular. Maybe the circle expands as you practice. And Jan's view supports the familiar phrase, "What goes around comes around."

A particular day comes to mind in which I faced disappointment from several quarters: important calls missed, mail absent a promised payment, news of another economic failure here in our own democracy. These disappointments cast an interesting light on my understanding of Maugham's words and Jan's assertion. Repeatedly, I have seen what I thought was "the best thing" turn out to be the worst possible choice. I have also determined, well in advance of an event, my sense of how it would go in the best scenario and have been utterly taken in delight by something completely different than I anticipated. As my housemate and I strategized about and anticipated our next home, I found myself setting aside specifics, an unusual step for me, and advocating that I hoped for a few specifics but would let the rest unfold. With the push-push-push of a specific and rigid agenda, the "best" can accidentally be rejected when it shows up... because it does not look like or meet the identified set of expectations.

So I held a loosely framed set of hopes and moved into a home that far exceeded what I had imagined. I am reminded in so many ways that to live as if this is all there is allows the circumstances of the day to present themselves as the best the day has to offer. In turn, I aspire to offer my best to the day. And that seems to draw a beneficial circle. Some call this a virtuous circle.

Recognize the Value in the Priorities of Others

I can stop to see you. I am able to pause what I am doing to see what is important to you. Recently, while visiting the California Academy of Sciences, I saw a mom taking a photo of her two daughters. "Would you like to be in the picture?" "Oh, yes!" she said as she handed me her camera without hesitation. Two lovely daughters, an enthused mom, and two disinterested stuffed zebras later, I handed her digital camera back. She looked with approval at the image that registered immediately. "Oh, that's good. Thank you." I returned to my cadence and to a friend who said, "That's a mitzvah." *Mitzvah* brought to mind the lyrical recitation, "No sadness, no sadness. It is a mitzvah to forget the gloom."

A mitzvah. A good deed performed out of a sense of religious or spiritual duty. The definition differs and expands for me: a mitzvah is a positive act intended as an investment in goodness and joy—both my own and others.

A Single Generosity Enlarges the World

One bold inspiration choreographs a dance with promise. One unlikelihood entertained leads a parade of innovation. One whispered yes becomes the wind song over an ocean of noes. One service to need heals an ancient wound. One movement toward light becomes a clear signpost on a long road. A small compassionate act enlarges the scope of community. Teachers or any professionals might be tempted to ask if their purpose on the planet might be a level deeper than originally thought. An initial thought is we are here to inspire many others. What if it's really to inspire the few who will, in turn, inspire the many? Or more to the point, to influence one who will in turn change the world. Today may be that day: your one day to have that single most important influence on the life of another human being.

***

Judgment and weariness are foes to service and generosity.

In service, there is clarity and compassion to override these two forces of negativity. Judgment is discernment on a bad hair day. Weariness comes, on some days, from lack of service to self. When I was finished pouring my heart into a presentation, I was supposed to be signing books. More to the point, the host of the event expected me to be selling books. So many people wanted to engage me with their questions and tell their stories. I had to make a choice. I listened to the stories. Would these same people have been compelled to tell these very same stories to any speaker who had addressed them? I will never know. I only know that they chose to tell me, and I stood still. I set down my commercial obligations, and I served the souls who had stories to tell. I listened as one woman wove her story. And what an amazing story she told: a lost child, a broken dream followed by a dream realized, art discovered. And on August 21, 1968, Russian tanks roared into Prague, changing her life forever. In 1973, she emigrated to her freedom in America. On Thanksgiving Day. I still hear her words ringing in my ears, "The first Thanksgiving here in the US served all who were immigrants. Many Americans do not know or have forgotten what it is to come here new. That was a real Thanksgiving for me in 1973, and it is, every year since." I could have judged the talking ones to be at odds with my requirements. My weariness could have cut short my capacity to entertain the "next" story. With those foes set aside, I listened. And every Thanksgiving since is a richer experience for that listening.

Just How Busy Are You?

Greetings to You,

You always hear from me, but I thought I'd officially notify you today on behalf of expectation, uncertainty, self-recrimination, and resistance. We are involved in a significant meeting. Since everybody knows me as the Busy Mind, they figured asking me to do "one more thing" wouldn't matter. "Bring it on! I can do it all—even though I already have so much to do." Yes. That's really me talking when those self-martyring phrases come out of your mouth. Well, anyway, I'm speaking on their behalf today. Left to your own devices, you just play with delight and create from your heart. Thank God! I'm here to remind you of all your responsibilities, strengths, and shortcomings. See, I try for balance in my whispering. No wonder you've been tucking your head into those little electronic word games. You can't hear me there. It really bugs me when you do that, by the way. When you come out of the soundproof booth, I have to up my game just to bring you up to speed.

Look, it's our collective jobs to keep you connected to everything. All that "letting go" stuff you practice just keeps us all damn busy running around, catching the stuff, and bringing it back to you. If you'd just hold onto stuff in the first place, it would make all of our jobs so much easier. (You're just lucky I haven't endorsed a union here. You would really have a hard time shutting us out then.) Just keep in mind that we are committed—we will do whatever it takes to keep you mired in our realities. I wish you'd give up this focus phrase process of yours. That's another thing that makes our jobs super hard.

How's a busy mind supposed to be effective when your mind is open, at ease, and simply observing and learning from the world around you? I'm the conduit. I want to be in charge, and I want you to let me be in charge.

Yeah, yeah, everybody—I know! Everybody here wants to think that they are in charge. Fine. You all can think what you want. Okay, okay, I'll communicate on their behalf now.

Fear says he's only trying to protect you from making the same mistakes.

Hey, wait a minute! Fear, when did you show up to this meeting? I hate it when you slip in late without me noticing.

Expectation says she's only trying to help you live up to your astonishingly well-polished standard trophies. Uncertainty reminds you he's actually creativity in disguise—but he doesn't want you to get all soft and cushy in your career, so he dresses up as uncertainty. (You know this already, right? Seriously? How do you forget a thing like that? Maybe I've fallen down on my job by not helping you remember this.)

About self-recrimination: before I let you hear from that department, let me just say that self-recrimination has been a real management challenge for me. She often steps in trying to do my job. Imagine. Her! Trying to sound like the Busy Mind. But she's actually been pulling it off quite a bit lately. So help me watch out for that, okay? All right. Self-recrimination, my underling, my employee, self-recrimination, who reports first to me, not to you—just wants you to know she knew you before everybody else. She knew you when you were just an obscure nobody. Who would keep you humble if she didn't?

Resistance is the head of the Internal Corps of Engineers. He's very busy right now so he left right after we started this meeting. But I can tell you what's what. He understands your lack of artistic discipline.

He sees how you've succumbed to the process of designing by fire—large bonfire bursts. So he just steps in and digs those fire line trenches as deep as he can. By the time the fire is large enough to breach the line, it is roaring and unstoppable.

I know. I know. It leaves you exhausted. But that's one of my busiest times. I get to keep you engaged with all the other things you haven't done while creative fire building. See? We really do all work hard for you. So if you could stop this being present with the present moment in a state of joy nonsense, it would go a lot better for all of us. There is so much more I could say—but I've got a lot to do, so I've got to go. Take care.

With earnest regard,

—The Busy Mind

Enlist in the Company of Angels

Seen or unseen, there is, indeed, a world of grace that exists alongside my own. I give little study and much gratitude to the world of otherness. I recognize the angels on the road in my experiences. I neither define nor defend them.

On my most contented, centered days, I sense an almost playful exchange with this company of beings. And on other days, I am embarrassed at my acknowledgment of this presence of unseen others. It is not academic. It is not particularly demonstrable, but by anecdotal tale. I can't open a cupboard to present my collection of angels nor can I prescribe a meeting place or schedule their appearance in my planning book. No, I find them only when I am open in my heart to the holy opportunity of a single precious moment.

***

*"We shall never know all the good
that a simple smile can do."*

—Mother Teresa

The first good we can know is the good that it does for us—for those of us who are offering the smile. Smiling changes perspective. A smile changes each encounter to a greater likelihood of joy or possibility or at least something pleasant. My smile can come readily, but today it wasn't simply an unconscious response. I smiled at everyone today because I was reflecting on Mother Teresa's phrase. It turned out to be the equivalent to an all-day pass to everyone's gates. I spoke at length with several strangers—and even a few dogs, too.

I have no way of knowing, with any certainty, the good that my all-day smiles did for others. I know without a doubt what good it did for me.

Future Value

My years in business were a fascinating companion to my life as an artist. My closest friends would watch lovingly, bemused and sometimes amazed at how my poet-self navigated the practical requirements of my role as a leader in my own company. I remember a meeting with two key advisors, my corporate accountant and my corporate attorney. The accountant spoke to me of best practices and conventional wisdom. He instructed that I must speculate on future value—the future value of this enterprise that was born of my passion, my intention, and years of hard work. Inside, I politely disagreed. As I sat in that office, I knew the only value I could genuinely measure, yes, the only "value" of any value to me was held in this particular moment—*this* now. I know they continued to talk. And I'm sure I missed some salient points. Yet what I remember to this day was a different measure of my own wealth than the one that their particular skills were offering to me.

We are not generous because we are wealthy, but because we are abundant. We do not give because we have extra, we share because we have enough.

Artful Intention

The in-between times are some of the hardest times in life: no marching bands, no parade. There is no grand event to either plan or attend. These liminal spaces, called thresholds by some, are filled with waiting and plenty of temptation to ask, "What's next?" Turns out the next right thing on such days is simply showing up—showing up to the promises that have been made, watering the garden that you planted at the beginning of the season that hasn't begun showing any signs of growth yet. Yet. Maybe it is more true that what feels like "in between" is the actual stuff of life: the diligence without the drama, the ordinary fulfillment, acting from the fundamental roots that produce the expressions of our lives…the branches, the blossoms, and the leaves. It turns out that doing that which is ordinary with intention and mindfulness may be at the core of the most satisfying and artful life.

It is a welcome contradiction that it is in the narrative of history that I find the best case for living as if this is all there is. We know so much about the everyday life of the residents of Herculaneum and Pompeii only because they didn't know that in moments they would be preserved for posterity by the volcanic eruptions of Vesuvius.

I have gathered rocks from every place I have traveled. I have searched long stretches of sand for shells on many different shores.

Both stones and shells speak both of longevity and the transitory nature of a thing. Long in the making, a shell provides a dwelling for a period of time for a succession of sea creatures. In their form, I find a case for treasuring the moment that is here and now and am able to hold it in my hand.

Message in a Shell

A shell, both unique and common, without bearing the burden of contradiction, is evidence of beauty, a currency of timelessness. In an impulse that transcends all epochs, I gather: the broken as beautiful as the whole, the imperfect more interesting than the perfect. Washed, set to dry in the sun, these collective memories are contained now, domesticated, held in an Irish crystal bowl. Someday, someone will wonder at the story of these architectural remnants. Perhaps these shells will find their way, as I always have, back to the wild and unfettered sea.

Here There Be Dragons

In the work I've developed to help me remember and do what matters, I identify four key elements of priority. *And* I always leave a space for the fifth, which most often I label, "Here There Be Dragons." That is how medieval cartographers designated the lands beyond their knowing. In the most practical of terms, our known intentions, the ones held deeply, are still not able to reach and identify the place on our map called "the future." Tolkien wisely wrote that it's not any good to make plans or calculations without including a dragon if you happen to live anywhere near one. Intentions are our map. They represent the core cartography of each of our souls. And the future? It is a mystery that we enter one step, one second at a time.

What you carry, how you travel, and the reasons why you have established those intentions determine the nature of your steps. This is why there is power in the suggestion that you remember, and do what matters.

Watch What You Carry

Rise up and watch what you carry.
Can you not see your burden?
Listen to the stories you tell.
Listen to the tales you carry,
set down and pick up, set down and pick up again.
You are your story.
The words you weave become your garments.
The words you weave become your carpet.
The words you weave are your meal, they are your drink,
they become your liver, your lips, your life.
Rise up, creature, and watch what you carry.
Can you see the road before you?
Listen to the invitation of your soul.
You do not have to travel just because there is a road.
If it is not your journey you may stay.
Rest. Sit a while.
They are your feet—only go where they wish to carry you.
They must not walk a road that belongs to someone else.
Rise up and watch what you carry.
Can you love the wind that blew you here
without insisting it take you further?
Can you thank the warp of your days

without asking it to be on a larger frame?
Can you intend to live with a contradiction
between the acceptance of the is
right beside the possibility of the if? Rise Up.
Rise up.
Rise up, step into the next mystery
and watch what you carry.

Part II

Remember and Do What Matters

Being busy.

Doing what matters.

These two things are often confused with one another. We know at an intuitive level which things matter most to us. And for some of the busiest people, all that is required is to look at the list they are working from and see what keeps getting shuffled to the bottom of that list! Why is that?

There are fundamental assumptions that the things that matter most are going to be the most difficult, require the most expertise, or cost more than your available resources. They are the items that get put in the category of "When I have time, I'm gonna…" Do you have a blank like this to fill in? How many times do you hear yourself or a friend of yours say, "I spent the whole day doing stuff, yet it feels like I did nothing." Maybe that sentence could be amended to, "It feels like I did nothing that really mattered."

Some days, that is an accidental truth.

Because I spent my teenage years largely without adult supervision, I earnestly sought out systems that helped me manage through the various requirements to adulthood. Certainly my circle of fine young friends made an indelible mark on the way I navigated my days. Beyond that, I would parent myself. I would ask questions that I imagined a caring parent would ask me. Those questions were tied to when things were due, what was essential to tend my own health care needs, what would make me feel good or successful or happy, and what would help me learn to manage something I didn't know how to do. This method of inquiry prepared me for an early career as a consultant with nonprofit agencies. I assisted low- to mid-level staff members in establishing management systems that aligned with their personal styles of work. I used the techniques I'd learned in the second decade of my life, methods of inquiry that allowed them to have unique and measurable insight into their own best practices. Essentially, I helped them remember their way back to their most natural, productive state. Many of the people I got to work with were so frustrated because they were using time and information management systems that had been handed to them with the information that these were efficient and productive ways of getting things done and a request to please adjust themselves accordingly. One system cannot outfit every single person in an organization to optimize their time and choose their most significant priorities first. It's personal. And it can change over time.

How do you look at the mulch of your life and allow the must to rise up? What clarity can be applied to the many things that you are indeed able to do to enable you to focus in on the things you really want to do, those things which will most dramatically access your core values and intentions and will produce results that make your heart sing?

When you remember and make daily choices based upon what most matters to you—those decisions become so much clearer.

I've guided hundreds of people through a process that, no surprise, is called "*Remember and Do What Matters.*" I make that entire curriculum available to you here. You might use it with a friend or an accountability partner and share your responses. You could treat it as the prompt for a weekly study group or allow the prompts to guide conversation in a book group. I guide this process periodically with personalized commentary and exchange. In any event, I suggest that you write your responses and keep them in a single document to make the review of your responses more convenient. They are progressive and intended to be completed in the order they are written. I expect you could imagine many ways to pursue this material. At the end of the matter, it's likely that you will have insights you could not have predicted and will hold in your hand a relevant manifesto of the way that you want to intentionally approach the days of your life. And along the way, it's possible that you will enjoy a deeper understanding of the core intentions that propel you on your journey.

Here you go. Enjoy your experience as you remember and do what matters.

One

In your home or in your yard, go to one of your favorite things or places, a thing or place that brings you a lot of joy. It can be as small as a piece of jewelry or as large as a tree in your yard. Got it?

Think about the reasons why you chose this particular thing or place in your home or yard as something that brings you a lot of joy. Then, sometime today between now and when you go to bed, have that thing or place write *you* a letter! Personify it—and allow all that you imagine of it to stir your imagination. Write down what you think it would write you—if it could. Be sure to allow it to mention within the letter what elements about the thing or place are that bring you joy.

Two

Imagine this...

Through a peculiar set of events, you *know* right now that just before bedtime tonight...you are going to lose your memory for six weeks.

You'll still be fundamentally "you," but for six weeks you'll have absolutely no long-term memories stored. (Isn't it great that this imaginary exercise ends with you getting your full capacity back?)

Imagine that for support in this six-week time period, you will gather five iconic things that will be accompanied by a note. The things will be a visual prompt to remind you of who you are…and the note that you write will provide a brief explanation of why each icon is important to you. Here's my example:

My five things: a blank book, a fine point pen pack, a dictionary, a photo of my favorite group of humans, and some stamped, unaddressed envelopes. The blank book is an invitation to discover significant truths through writing (you are a writist); the fine point pen pack allows you to rainbow-mark your world with form and word (you are an artist); the dictionary allows you to come to most any word explanation that you will need (you are a learner); you hold the friends in your circle as beloveds (you are a fine friend); and you love to encourage and uplift others with mail (you enjoy inspiring people).

Please look around you. Choose what five icons would best remind you of what really matters to you in this imagined time of memory loss. Write a note about them.

Three

Your body hears and believes everything you say to it—everything you say to yourself. Notice how you speak to yourself; notice how you talk to yourself about your body. Let your body write you a letter expressing its feelings and opinions regarding how you speak to it and how you treat it.

What are some ways to notice how you use self-talk?

Self-talk and the language used to talk to ourselves and our bodies is second nature to such a degree that it can be difficult to notice it. Here are ways to pay attention:

- Make an actual written note when you notice making any kind of comment to yourself, in the quiet of your own mind. After a period of some hours on the same day, look at the notes you made, and let that inform the letter you help your body write to you.

- When you wake up, do you have an awareness of your body and how you feel in it? Perhaps without even realizing it, that groan and impulse to roll over…are messages to your body. Or do you wake right up and jump out of bed? When you are choosing your clothing, do you make an assessment about how the clothes fit you or how your body looks in your clothes? If you have occasion to stretch, reach, or bend down to pick something up—do you experience gratitude for how nimble your body might be, or do you perhaps compare your physical ability to that of someone else or maybe a younger version of yourself?

These are some ways we "talk" to our body. Hopefully this awareness will enable you to let your body talk back to you in a letter today. *What* do you *imagine* your body would really want you to know?

Four

Let enthusiasm write you a letter evaluating how your brain and your body respond when they/you feel enthusiastic, specifically including *what* kinds of things generate an enthusiastic response. It may help if you look up the definition or etymology of the word "enthusiasm."

Five

Your environment tells you a lot about what matters to you.

She realized her life was a lot sweeter than she originally thought. Those sweet simple things managed to escape her notice in the press of her worries and obligations and commitments. However, once she allowed herself to start noticing…she discovered two, then four. Then they seemed to multiply daily. Noticing the simple things that bring joy seems to magically make room for more joy. Yay!

Fourteen

Make a list of all of the things that you dread in the course of this day.

Notice how your experience is different between exploring your inner self through the method of a letter versus making the inquiry through list-making.

To make this sort of list may require a different level of attentiveness to your experience throughout your day.

Fifteen

In the course of the day, you will/may experience some things that elicit a *strong reaction*…that reaction could be described as longing, passion, or conviction. Make a list of those things which drew out from you such strong feelings and/or reactions.

Sixteen

Imagine that you died at 103 doing something that you really loved doing. Write the eulogy for your life, exited at age 103, and include the things for which you really want to be remembered and celebrated. For the years between now and 103, you'll need to employ your best imagination!

Seventeen

Begin the process of creating your metric—connect the dots.

Read through your collected document. Begin to identify general categories (like Family, Learning, Justice, Community, Hospitality, or Travel, just as examples). Then begin distilling the patterns into smaller categories.

You are looking for four primary categories.

As you read through your writings, looking for your patterns, perhaps category titles will be apparent to you. If not, you can group them, A-B-C-D or 1-2-3-4, or else use color marks and place similar things together.

Don't worry, the category titles will show up. They are rooted in your deepest intentions.

Eighteen

Continue the process of evaluating your writing, identifying the patterns, and categorizing key elements. If you are completing this process with an accountability partner, a friend, or in a group, this is a good time to speak with each other. Share your processes for how you are reviewing and categorizing things.

Pay special attention to the writing you did on day two—the five things that you would gather as iconic reminders. There is a real key to what your categories might be in that day's writing. There is rich fodder for identifying what matters to you in *all* of your writings. I've said for decades, "We tell the tale of our lives by the stories we repeat in our days."

Nineteen

You will perhaps see the four categories emerge. And within those four *main* categories may be relevant or related things that are not the main emphasis, but are still important to you. **These are subcategories**. I recommend picking three.

Examples? Under my **Requirements** category: earning/investing, promises, and grit/perseverance. In my **Inspire** category, you'll find: write, make, and incite. This next one was a struggle for me. I am a lifelong learner; beyond that, I am curious and inquisitive. So my third category, which I *thought* was going to be learning, turned out to be **Inquire**: community, learn, and travel. Initially, I imagined travel was going to be one of my four categories. Upon further evaluation, I realized what I so love about travel is the opportunity to be in a different culture and learn about it and from it.

Identifying these subcategories helps you use this metric as a measure for what you say *yes* to and what you decline. The more specific you can be, the more helpful your metric will be.

Twenty

Consider **visuals** for which you have an affinity that can have four segments: a road with four lanes, a ruler with four primary segments, a tree with four main branches, a compass, and so on.

Create a visual representation of the categories and elements you have identified. This is a great opportunity to test out your visuals on the circle of people in your life who know you best; getting feedback is a fascinating aspect to this particular discovery.

Think of the visual in this way: it's like a logo for a business. When you see certain logos, you immediately know through the images what matters to that company. Consider that as you develop a visual that reflects your categories.

Twenty-One

In a single sentence, create a master statement that incorporates what you have remembered about doing what matters…

I remember and do what matters by

_____,

_____,

_____

and _____.

Twenty-Two

Express, in writing, how you imagine *remembering* these things that *matter* to you will impact your ability to act upon them and actually DO them. Tell me *where* you will put your physical metric and how you will reference your one-sentence reminder.

Here are some ideas regarding the processes that can be used to evaluate the responses you have written to these various inquiries.

Begin Pulling Your Observations Together!

Read over everything you have written since day one. Take notes on the patterns you observe and the types of things that you have repeated. This is a day of research on the most fascinating subject—you!

Some participants have used technology to create a Word Cloud process. Caren Albers shared that she, "did a word search in my Remember and Do writings to see important patterns of repetition that might hold clues to investigate. You can count all things, but all things don't count in my world. Similar to Einstein's remark, "Many of the things you can count, don't count. Many of the things you can't count really count."

You can use colored pens to make a mark by a certain category or highlight it.

You are essentially distilling a lot of information down to a little.

You might imagine that my processes have changed, morphed, and altered over the years. However, the four categories have largely remained the same. I return to this practice each year. It's like an annual check-up!

As you practice what you learn from the Remember and Do What Matters process, you will be able to look at what fills up your days and weeks…and say yes to what you must. To live your days with intention is to live them with your heart fully engaged with what matters most.

This process can be repeated annually or every few years. Things change. And what matters most now may not have the same relevance some time from now. In my own process, the primary categories which reflect my core intentions have remained largely the same. How I explain them is what changes over the years. As you root yourself more deeply in the clarified and better understood intentions of your life, decisions come more cleanly and with greater specificity.

Opportunities that are grand in scope can be passed by...because you can know they are opportunities for someone besides you. Things that seem beyond your imagination can be embraced, because you know they align with what matters to you. May clarity and deepened understanding be your companions as you grow and thrive in your intentional life.

Acknowledgements

To my readers and those who tend what I write and make, thank you. You allow me the privilege of earning my livelihood with work about which I am passionate and committed. I would not be able to do this without you.

Brenda Knight, how fortunate I am that you keep wanting to see the books I've got in me. Thanks to you and Mango Publishing for helping me continue to live with intention and write to find the meaning in these days.

There are many individuals who have contributed to the impact of this book, and their reflections begin each of my chapters.

Bo Mackison guides a contemplative practice that I enjoy. BoMackison.com.

Linda Bannan and I happily learn and create things together.

Pat Wiederspan Jones is an artist and a teacher of fine art. Her work populates my home, museums, and galleries.

Kim Jayhan's story is impactful, and I'm glad it is told on these pages.

Bev Jones's playfulness is epitomized in her colorful contributions in her community.

Jean Martell is committed to kindness, and her tender view toward the world is shown in the photographic work she sells and shares.

Dr. Steve Maraboli inspires countless thousands of people with his stories and wisdom—including me. SteveMaraboli.net.

Caren Albers, the author of *Happiness Junkie* and *Married to a Vegan*, is someone I admiringly call a Clarity Ninja.

Arla DeField enthusiastically builds jewelry, travels the country, and guides accountability groups. Numbers of her books are available on Amazon, including *Mastering the Art of Saying No Without Feeling Guilty* and *Jewelry Making: Tips & Tricks of the Trade.*

Pam Matchie-Thiede inspires wildly creative living and assists others to living healthier lives. Learn more about her at PamMatchie.com.

Dr. Kymn Rutigliano is a tenured professor in the field of leadership and contributes to numbers of academic and nonfiction works.

Sue Robson is a licensed practitioner with the Center for Spiritual Living and articulates many of her practices at PrayerMalas.com.

Robert Ruder is a professor at Gonzaga University. As a Social Architect, he creates opportunities to better understand the systems that propel our lives. Learn more about his work at RobertRuder.com.

I relate a story by a longtime peer, Bonnie Rae Nygren. If you are curious about her stories, you can find her at insearchofthevery.com.

You'll read references to many people in this book that you have likely never heard of before. I take some of the best life lessons from my friends, and that is how it comes to be that you read about so many of them here.

Robbie Hanson continues to apply his greatly appreciated team building skills, and I am grateful to continue to learn from him. My MindHive has lifted me with great ideas and given loft to a career that had already made me very happy. I am grateful to be surrounded by old and new friends as I continue to live my life with intention.

This book is an easier read thanks to the studied eyes of my friends Connie Bennett and Barbara Grassey.

P.S.

It's amusing to think back the many years to my first book. I remember resisting the practice of featuring endorsements for me and the book. I insisted that people should be able to make up their own minds without being influenced by reviews. Certainly my experience has changed my mind. Reviews are just like cost comparisons and spreadsheets...they help us to know what something does and what it does not do. If this book has done something of value for you, I'd be honored if you would take the time to share that in a review. There are many platforms, Amazon and Goodreads among them. And if there is something you believe I can do better, I'd like to hear from you at maryanneradmacher.net/connect-with-me.

Perhaps even more significant that formal reviews are the recommendations that friends offer other friends. Or the gifts that you choose to offer people in your circle of influence. If you find value in these words I have composed, I would be grateful to you for any of the ways that you would choose to share them with others.

Thanks for holding this book in your hands. And should you be inspired to do so, thanks for sharing your inspiration with others.

About the Author

Mary Anne Radmacher is a writer and an artist who applies her decades of experience in the business world to working with her consulting clients. She teaches online courses and workshops on living a full, creative, and balanced life. She has been writing and using her writing to explore symbols and find meaning since she was a child.

She considers the respect of her peers and the friendships she holds to be among the special honors she has received in her lifetime. She's enjoyed creating original work for people around the globe. Honored to have edited *Be Brave* and *Chase Your Dreams* on behalf of former President Clinton, she is the author of (among others) *Lean Forward Into Your Life*, *Live Boldly*, and *Life Begins When You Do*. She is the coauthor with Jonathan Lockwood Huie of *Simply an Inspired Life: Consciously Choosing Unbounded Happiness in Good Times and Bad* and contributed significantly to Marci Moore's *Love Letters from Your Life: Inspired Ways to Show Up with Love*.

Find out more about her at: maryanneradmacher.net.

Mango Publishing, established in 2014, publishes an eclectic list of books by diverse authors—both new and established voices—on topics ranging from business, personal growth, women's empowerment, LGBTQ studies, health, and spirituality to history, popular culture, time management, decluttering, lifestyle, mental wellness, aging, and sustainable living. We were recently named 2019 *and* 2020's #1 fastest growing independent publisher by *Publishers Weekly*. Our success is driven by our main goal, which is to publish high quality books that will entertain readers as well as make a positive difference in their lives.

Our readers are our most important resource; we value your input, suggestions, and ideas. We'd love to hear from you—after all, we are publishing books for you!

Please stay in touch with us and follow us at:

Facebook: Mango Publishing
Twitter: @MangoPublishing
Instagram: @MangoPublishing
LinkedIn: Mango Publishing
Pinterest: Mango Publishing

Newsletter: mangopublishinggroup.com/newsletter

Join us on Mango's journey to reinvent publishing, one book at a time.